THE UNIVERSAL CODE OF

(Formerly)

UNWRITTEN RULES

From *AIRLINE-ARMREST ETIQUETTE*
to *FLUSHING TWICE*,
251 Uncompromising Laws of Common
Civility That We Wish Everyone Knew

QUENTIN PARKER

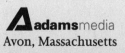

Avon, Massachusetts

Published by
Adams Media, a division of F+W Media, Inc.
57 Littlefield Street, Avon, MA 02322. U.S.A.
www.adamsmedia.com

ISBN 10: 1-4405-1225-6
ISBN 13: 978-1-4405-1225-4
eISBN 10: 1-4405-2730-X
eISBN 13: 978-1-4405-2730-2

Printed in the United States of America.

10   9   8   7   6   5   4   3   2   1

Library of Congress Cataloging-in-Publication Data
is available from the publisher.

This publication is designed to provide accurate and authoritative information with regard to the subject matter covered. It is sold with the understanding that the publisher is not engaged in rendering legal, accounting, or other professional advice. If legal advice or other expert assistance is required, the services of a competent professional person should be sought.

—From a *Declaration of Principles* jointly adopted by a Committee of the American Bar Association and a Committee of Publishers and Associations

Many of the designations used by manufacturers and sellers to distinguish their product are claimed as trademarks. Where those designations appear in this book and Adams Media was aware of a trademark claim, the designations have been printed with initial capital letters.

This book is available at quantity discounts for bulk purchases.
For information, please call 1-800-289-0963.

CONTENTS

INTRODUCTION

It has been nearly a century since the publication of Emily Post's 1922 classic, *Etiquette in Society, in Business, in Politics, and at Home*. Much of her volume seems laughably quaint today, with its focus on which servants should perform which tasks in which rooms and its stipulation that you bow (!!) to your friends rather than tip your hat to them. Nonetheless, Ms. Post is sorely missed today.

Not *everyone* has forgotten his or her manners, though, at times, you'd be hard-pressed to find anyone who remembers that it really is important to be nice and courteous. If you're reading this book, then you're one of us. We are the twenty-first-century individuals who believe it's even more important to bring civility than it is to bring sexy back. Heck, courtesy *is* sexy because it makes us look more attractive.

Everyone complains about how uncivilized Americans are, yet many of these complainers are regularly committing uncouth acts of their own. Rather than assume they're complete jerks (which is probably *not* a safe assumption), we'll assume that they just don't know the rules. What rules? The mostly unwritten rules we should follow in society, in business, and at home (screw politics—it's inherently and irredeemably vicious). *Those* rules.

What? You don't know those rules? Well, of course you don't. I just told you they're unwritten. But you're in luck! You hold in your hands the key to the future of a civilized nation (and you just thought it was a humor book you could keep on top of the toilet tank). This book contains the unwritten rules everyone should follow. These are rules that, if followed, will ensure that you are not viewed by your friends, lovers, and co-workers as benighted trailer trash.

You won't find commands to bow to friends or directions for chambermaid duties in the following pages, but you will find advice and instruction about the proper way to practice etiquette in the twenty-first century and beyond. Ms. Post might not like this volume's occasionally snarky tone nor its sporadic use of coarse language, but I'd like to think she would approve of its spirit.

CHAPTER 1

UNWRITTEN RULES

ON THE ROAD

We love our automobiles because they give us our own individual fiefdoms within which we are undisputed kings and queens. That's why we act like we own the road. That's why we get so angry when other motorists disrespect us. That's why we dehumanize other drivers, thinking of *their* cars as obstacles and not as vehicles being piloted by other human beings.

The problem with this vehicular superiority complex is that it leads to rampant incivility on the roads. A license to drive becomes a license to be a douche. Chances are, if you leave your driveway, someone will do *something* that transforms you from gentle soul to raging, homicidal-maniac wannabe.

Granted, many of the "unwritten rules" in the following section are not, in fact, unwritten. Yet they're blatantly, flagrantly, and egregiously ignored anyway. Consequently, it's important to draw your attention to these unwritten and written rules, just to make sure that you're not being a menace to society.

MAKE A TURN FOR THE BETTER

The use of turn signals is a forgotten art, like that guy who used to spin plates on sticks on old, black-and-white variety shows. No, that's incorrect. Turn signals have been ignored since they first arrived in vehicles. If covered wagons had them, they wouldn't have been used in the Wild West either.

That thing sticking out of the left side of your steering column? It's not just for show. It's not an *objet d'art*. It's a turn signal, genius, and you should *always* use it to signal a turn. That's why it's there.

Even though you (believe that you) have an incredible mind, it cannot be read by other drivers. When you stop suddenly in the middle of the road without using a turn signal, you're risking one of the following: A) Pissing off other drivers. B) A fiery crash. C) Being called a "prick"—or worse—by other drivers. D) All of the above.

UNWRITTEN RULE #1: One should always use a turn signal to indicate that one is turning.

SEE THE LIGHTS?

Funerals are sad observations of loss. So, why do you want to make things worse for those already grieving? You say you would never do possibly cut into a funeral procession; that you are fully aware of the solemnity of the occasion. We say, "Bull."

Wasn't that you who cut off that funeral procession because you were in such a hurry to get to Wal-Mart? Wal-Mart! Trust us, they can take your money a few minutes later. If you think your petty errands are more important than the needs of a dead person's family and friends, then there is something seriously wrong with you.

If you notice that a group of cars is moving more slowly than you would like, check for telltale signs: cars in the line with lights on in broad daylight, hearses, etc. If you see these things, do not interfere with the procession of vehicles unless you or someone in your car is hemorrhaging.

UNWRITTEN RULE #2: One should always be respectful of funeral processions and not interfere with their progress.

GREEN MEANS GO

The civilized man has built a coach but has lost the use of his feet.
—RALPH WALDO EMERSON

While many people, as just noted, are not familiar with the equation red means stop, an equal number are not familiar with the equation's obverse: green means go.

Let us focus in on the habits of this species, *Dweebie zumdoofus.*

You are the fifth or sixth car sitting at a left turn signal, so you are concerned you will not make it through the light. Wait for it . . . wait for it. There! Green! But the—let's just call her an unpleasant person—at the head of the line doesn't move. She's texting or fumbling with her mp3 player or applying lipstick in the rearview mirror or some damn thing. What she's not doing is *going through the freaking green light.*

UNWRITTEN RULE #3: One should always be extremely vigilant when waiting for a stoplight to turn green.

DON'T GET HORNY

Any man who can drive safely while kissing a pretty girl is simply not giving the kiss the attention it deserves.
—ALBERT EINSTEIN

Even if someone has broken the "green means go" rule, you should be careful about laying on your horn. For one thing, the driver may look mild-mannered, but your horn could supply the shot across the bow that turns accountant into golf club–wielding psychopath.

For another, the horn is a safety device. A tractor trailer appears dead set on spreading the entrails of you and your car's occupants all over the street? Use the horn. A child whose parents haven't taught her basic traffic safety is chasing a ball into the street? Use the horn. Some dazed commuter is taking a second or two to start moving at the green light? Nope.

UNWRITTEN RULE #4: One should use one's horn sparingly and only as a safety device.

DON'T DRIVE BLINDLY

Being a sober, civilized sort, you put on your blinker and prepare to merge into an adjacent lane. You've checked your mirrors, and all systems are go. You begin to merge, only to hear the blast of a horn, and—just like that—you've wet yourself (again!).

Two unwritten rules are at work in this instance. The first is that you should always check your blind spot. That's the place where "ghost cars" lurk. Ghost cars are those vehicles that stealthily creep up beside you and then stay there, out of range of your side and rearview mirrors.

The second rule involves ghost cars. Don't be one. Never sit in someone's blind spot. If you do, you are—in addition to being considered a total idiot—flirting with disaster.

UNWRITTEN RULE #5: One should always check one's blind spot before changing lanes, and one should never drive in another motorist's blind spot.

TWO LANES, ONE DORK

Ah, a bucolic mountain road, sweeping past piney vistas. There's only one problem: that etiquette-lacking SOB in front of you, who's going ten miles an hour.

Two-lane roads often lack passing lanes or even dotted center lines. Consequently, your only hope for moving any faster is a motorist having the courtesy to pull into the shoulder so you can pass. However, you're more likely to witness a deer taking a smoke break than you are to see a fellow motorist with this degree of courtesy.

Perhaps the slow driver is trying to get you to slow down and smell the roses, or perhaps he's just a rude, thoughtless jerk. Either way, he—and all other denizens of scenic byways—need to get the heck out of the way.

UNWRITTEN RULE #6: If one is driving more slowly than other motorists on a two-lane road, one should pull into the shoulder to let the other motorists pass.

YOU'RE NOT A HOLOGRAM

The best car safety device is a rearview mirror with a cop in it.
—DUDLEY MOORE

Let's say you're going to leave a parking lot and want to peek out to see if any cars are coming. Oops, you've actually pulled *into* the road. Well, that's a simple fix. Just back up a little bit. Hey, wait a minute! Why are you still sticking out into the road? Apparently, you have no sense of self-preservation or, more likely, just no sense.

You are not spectral. Other cars cannot drive through you. If you remain out in the road, you could be T-boned by an equally unaware driver, or you could cause a vigilant driver to swerve into another lane and hit yet another innocent motorist. Just like that, you've involved three vehicles in a completely avoidable accident.

Don't be lazy/stupid/lacking in self-preservation. Back up, if you can. Next time, pay attention.

UNWRITTEN RULE #7: One should never pull out into the street and sit there, blocking traffic or causing an accident.

GET OUT OF THE DAMN SPACE

You've circled the lot for five minutes to no avail. If it weren't for the fact that little Tommy *needs* that hot new toy (which he'll play with for ten minutes then never pick up again), you'd just give up, go home, and crack open a cold one.

Ah, finally! That guy isn't just going to the trunk to put in more holiday gifts. He's actually getting behind the wheel! There he goes. Any second now . . .

And then nothing happens. He just sits there. Perhaps he has car trouble. Perhaps he's intoxicated. Most likely, he's relishing the small amount of power he possesses as long as he holds the space, knowing that you're waiting for it.

Pity him and his sad, miserable attempt at feeling important. In the meantime, don't attack him with a golf club. Just wait as patiently as possible, and he will move . . . eventually.

UNWRITTEN RULE #8: One should always vacate a parking space as quickly as possible.

LET PEOPLE OVER, YOU JERK

Once upon a time, a driver put on her left turn signal. A motorist in the other lane immediately slowed down in order to let her switch lanes, and both lived happily ever after.

This story shouldn't be a fairy tale, but, unfortunately, it is. In recent years, drivers have begun to treat turn signals like orders to speed up. Often, some drivers appear to practice a form of extra-sensory perception, speeding up in anticipation that someone *might* want to get in front of them.

Stop being in such a hurry. Your member won't shrivel up if someone gets in front of you.

UNWRITTEN RULE #9: If someone signals a desire to get in one's lane, one should always let him or her over.

IF YOU'RE IN A HURRY, DON'T SLOW ME DOWN

Here's a common occurrence that defies logic and reason. You're driving along, minding your own business, when someone pulls out in front of you only to drive twenty miles per hour slower than you were traveling. And what's worse, there's not another driver in sight behind you.

After you've measured admirable restraint and avoided shooting any etiquette-lacking hand gestures at the offending driver, your mind wanders: "Dang, if that guy's in such a hurry, then why is he slowing

8

me down? Why couldn't he have just waited until I passed since there's nobody behind me? Why does this always happen to me? Does calling lotion 'moisturizer' make me gay?"

UNWRITTEN RULE #10: One should never pull in front of a motorist and then drive slowly.

BACK OFF, BRO

Frankly, we can't remember the formula for how one determines a safe driving distance from the vehicle in front of you. We only know one thing: We should not be able to count your nose hairs in our rearview mirror.

Most people understand that it is impolite to violate someone's personal space, but they have no trouble doing this while behind the wheel of their Escalade, Hummer, Lexus, or other luxury car driven by people so rich that they believe that rules—written OR unwritten— do not apply to them. Oh, and let's not forget the other main class of too-close followers, the ones who would gladly drink the chewing tobaccoed-sputum of their favorite NASCAR driver. You're not Kevin Harvick, brother, so back off!

UNWRITTEN RULE #11: One should never follow another driver very closely. Always observe a safe and civil following distance.

LEFT = FAST

Grandma, we love you. We love your cute, rambling stories about life during the Depression when you had to use axle grease instead of butter and raw sewage instead of batter. We love the booties you knit us each year that we never use. But grandma, you just don't belong behind the wheel of that massive deathmobile any longer.

Case in point: Just because you intend to turn left in eighty miles does *not* mean that you should stay in the left lane during your entire trip. That lane is really for passing or for people with very good radar detectors who don't mind going well over the speed limit. It's not for you. When limping deer that have just been knocked over the hood of a car can move faster than you, you are driving too slowly. We really hate to tell you this, but it's true.

UNWRITTEN RULE #12: One should only use the left lane for passing or for driving really, really fast.

DON'T PASS THIS WAY AGAIN

The car has become the carapace, the protective and aggressive shell, of urban and suburban man.
—MARSHALL MCLUHAN, PHILOSOPHER

Traffic laws may differ slightly from state to state, city to city, county to county, but one law is constant: Pass on the left, not on the right.

What's that you ask? Why are all those people passing on the right? The answer is simple: They're uncultured, uncivilized, etiquette-lacking douche bags (pardon my French). Perhaps their mommies and daddies did not give them enough love and affection when they were young uncultured, uncivilized, etiquette-lacking douche bags.

Even if you prefer to remain uncivilized, keep in mind that people aren't expecting anyone to go roaring by them on the right. Therefore, they are not as likely to check carefully before easing into the right lane. Your incivility could make you roadkill.

UNWRITTEN RULE #13: One should always pass other motorists on the left and never on the right.

LIFE IN THE FAST (TOLL) LANE

If you live in most northern states, toll roads are a sucky fact of life. Therefore, if you make toll roads worse, then you are, by definition, a malevolent human being. One of the most malevolent things you can do is get in the express-pass lane *and try to pay cash.*

People have paid good money to get express passes because they want to "express" or "go as quickly as possible through the toll." You slow them down with your stupidity and thoughtlessness. Please, please, pay attention to the lane markings.

UNWRITTEN RULE #14: One should never try to pay cash in the fast-pass lane of a toll road.

DON'T LEAVE IT RUNNING ON EMPTY

Here's a quick way to lose friends and have only a negative influence on people: Borrow someone's car and then return it with an empty gas tank.

If you borrow someone's car, it goes without saying that you're inconveniencing her. She didn't *have* to let you borrow her car simply because you chose to ignore that pesky, but insistent, oil light until your engine exploded. You're not entitled. The right to borrow a friend's car does not appear anywhere in the Declaration of Independence or the Constitution or even the Bill of Rights.

If you return someone's car on empty, then you have not merely perpetrated a peccadillo. Nay. You have descended into the nadir of nastiness, the troughs of trailer trashiness, the pits of prickdom.

**UNWRITTEN RULE #15: One should always return
a borrowed car with a full tank of gas.**

TURN THAT $%!#% DOWN!

*The one thing that unites all human beings—regardless of age,
gender, religion, economic status, or ethnic background—is that,
deep down inside, we all believe that we are above-average drivers.*

—DAVE BARRY

You're all about your music. You think earthy diatribes about the mercurial ways of young ladies played with nuclear test-strength bass is just perfect for drive time. Well, guess what? The rest of the world doesn't want to hear it, okay?

We're not disparaging Weezy, you understand. He's just fine for your car or your home or your iPod. No, we're concerned with the fact that we don't share your taste. If your bombastic bass-driven beats can be heard over our poor, pitiful sound systems, then something is wrong.

Besides, dude. We've got kids in the car. We don't want them asking embarrassing questions such as, "What are bitches and hos, daddy?" So, when you're on the road, stopped at the ATM, or pumping gas into your ride, keep your music to yourself.

UNWRITTEN RULE #16: One should never play the music in one's car at a volume discernible by other motorists.

THE ROAD IS NOT A FREAKING SKI SLOPE

Slalom skiing is thrilling to watch, especially up close. To view slalom driving, on the other hand, can spark a heart attack or cause a man's testicles to shrivel to the size of raisins.

Yes, we get it. You're in a hurry, and we're in your way. However, that does not give you the right to treat us like skinny poles with little flags on them. That's not a pair of skis you're operating. It's a vehicle that weighs well over a ton, inversely proportionate to the size of your brain.

UNWRITTEN RULE #17: One should never "slalom" between lanes of traffic in order to jockey for position.

JUST MAKE THE DAMN TURN

Americans will put up with anything provided it doesn't block traffic.
—DAN RATHER

Left turns can be tricky; it's true. But right turns are pretty straightforward. Slow slightly, and brake into the turn. This is how one *should* make a right turn. Unfortunately, many drivers believe that they must come to a complete stop before making their (simple, straightforward) turn.

These people, a special breed, are called *morons* (though never to their faces, because that would be uncivilized).

Folks, if there is a shoulder, slow down in it. If there isn't a shoulder, a right turn does *not* require first coming to a halt in the middle of traffic. An ever-so-slight application of the brakes will do the trick.

UNWRITTEN RULE #18: One should never stop in the middle of traffic in order to make a right turn.

FACE FRONT!

Once upon a time, people pulled forward into parking spaces. This was an idyllic time, when lemonade springs ran past saltwater taffy trees and the scenario of gas costing more than a dollar or—hardy har har—two dollars was to be found only in the minds of devious science-fiction authors.

In recent years, people have begun backing into parking spaces. There you are following someone, thinking he has opted not to park in a particular space when he stops suddenly, his back-up lights flash on, and he's coming right toward you.

Then, you watch as he struggles to back into the space. He comes *thisclose* to hitting the cars on either side of his and winds up diagonal in the space. No one can get into or out of adjacent cars.

How did this trend start? Is it Californian? Martian? Is it something Europeans do after scarfing down scones or baguettes or whatever it is that Europeans eat? Are the people parking this way in possession of a huge rap sheet, which might necessitate a quick getaway? We have no idea. We just know that backing into a parking space is something one should never do.

UNWRITTEN RULE #19: One should always pull forward into a parking space. One should never back into a parking space.

CIVILITY IS OKAY AT THE CORRAL

Some grocery and department stores post signs in their parking lots warning customers that the store is not responsible for damage to vehicles caused by shopping carts. Why do carts cause damage? Because some people are lazy.

We understand that you've pushed that cart through labyrinthine aisles and dealt with other rude people who took the last of the three-for-one cans of SPAM. We feel your frustration at rising costs. We know your feet hurt.

But after you've finally finished your chore and you've loaded your car, do the decent thing. Don't leave the cart at the edge of your space because the cart corral is a whole twenty-five feet away. Reach deeply within yourself and find that iota of civility. Take the cart to the corral so that wayward winds won't blow your cart into some poor schmuck's nearly-paid-for Daihatsu. Better yet, take the cart back to the store.

UNWRITTEN RULE #20: One should always return one's shopping cart to the store or place it in the cart corral.

WRONG WAY IN THE LOT

Do you remember your childhood? Of course you do. Well, then, do you remember riding the bumper cars? The ride always had prominent signs warning all drivers to go in the same direction in order to avoid head-on collisions.

Then why, as an ersatz adult, are you going the wrong way down lanes in the shopping center?!? Even if you find a space, you won't be able to get into it without really inconveniencing someone else, and that's just not cool. Besides, you run a greater risk of hitting someone or something because people aren't expecting to see you barreling down the wrong way in the lot.

UNWRITTEN RULE #21: One should never ignore obvious directional cues—arrows, diagonal spaces, etc.—in a parking lot.

GIVE THEM SOME SPACE

Never lend your car to anyone to whom you have given birth.
—ERMA BOMBECK

Just because you are, technically, within the confines of a parking space does not mean that you should leave your car where it is and head in for your latest batch of white cheddar cheez puffs and Pabst Blue Ribbon Light.

Nobody else is going to buy that crap, so what's the rush? Don't leave your car crooked, because the person in the next space may not be able to get out of her space without making a fifty-two point turn . . . unless she gets so pissed that she just hits your car and drives off. If you leave your car *thisclose* to the next space, then that motorist will not be able to get into his car and may retaliate by keying your car, slashing your tires, or lying in wait and beating you to a pulp.

UNWRITTEN RULE #22: One should always park properly in a parking space, never crookedly or too close to adjacent cars.

DON'T BE A SPACE HOG

If your goddamn car is so awesome that you simply *must* park it cattycornered in two spaces, then we have advice for you: Don't drive the goddamn thing. Leave it at home, in a special climate-controlled garage. Let it be a museum piece, one with which you can awe your friends not only with your taste but with your clearly heftier bank-book (or heftier willingness to go into chronic debt).

Besides, we know you're not parking the car that way in order to keep it safe. You're parking it that way to show off to total strangers who are just trying to go the grocery store because they need some milk. You're pathetic, dude (sure, we're just jealous, but, so what, you are pathetic).

Park in *one* space at the outer limits of the lot, away from other cars, if you just can't bring yourself to park in the best-available single spot like a normal person. Finally, we must let you know that you don't fool us. We know that having such a massive, impressive car means that (to mix metaphors) below the belt you don't have much under the hood.

UNWRITTEN RULE #23: One should never park one's expensive car catty-cornered in two spaces, taking up both of them.

THAT WON'T MAKE THE LIGHT CHANGE ANY FASTER

Creep. Creep. Creep. Creep. Creep. Green!

Guess what? The fact that you kept creeping up to that red light had absolutely no impact on the traffic light cycle. All it did was make the drivers around you nervous and edgy. You're like those people who keep pushing the elevator button in the mistaken, perhaps insane, assumption that doing so will cause the elevator to appear faster (see Rule #54).

Stop advertising to everyone around you that you are a pushy, impatient moron. It's perfectly clear without you making an issue out of it.

UNWRITTEN RULE #24: One should always stop at the red light and remain stationary until the light turns green.

DON'T MAKE MISSING YOUR TURN OUR PROBLEM

The last person to get across [Boston] was yelling, "The British are coming! The British are coming!"
—LEWIS BLACK

Oh, dang, fellow driver. You intended to go straight at the intersection but found yourself in the left-turn-only lane. Sucks for you ... Hey, wait a minute! We're trying to go left, so why aren't you moving?!? Oh, that's right, because you're coarse and ill-mannered, the kind who would take a bite out of every piece of candy before returning it to the sampler. Listen, sir or ma'am, just because *you* made a mistake doesn't mean you have to have a negative impact on other people's lives.

Next time, just bite the bullet. Make the left turn, find a convenient place to make a (legal, of course) U-turn, and return to the intersection at which you made your *faux pas*.

UNWRITTEN RULE #25: One should never make missing a turn another driver's problem.

HERE'S WHAT IT MEANS, IDIOT

Yield (*yeeld*) v. Concede; give over; surrender or relinquish to the physical control of another.

That's what the red and white triangular sign means at the end of some off-ramps. In case the definition is still too difficult to grasp, we will simplify it for you: You can't go just because you want to go. If another car is coming, then you need to stop (or at least slow down), wait for it to pass, and then go.

Many people ignore these signs, and as a result, accidents, near accidents, or at least gratuitous cursing occur daily on our roadways.

UNWRITTEN RULE #26: One should always heed yield signs.

DON'T JUST SIT THERE! THE LIGHT'S RED!

Most communities allow motorists to turn right on red. Unfortunately, most communities also have their share of people who, for one reason or another, refuse to turn right on red, even when the street they're waiting to turn onto is completely free of traffic.

Perhaps they are foreign, and turning right on red in their home country leads to incarceration in a barbaric prison. Perhaps they are old and thus afraid to move unless explicitly urged to do so by a green light. Perhaps they are stupid or distracted by a cell phone . . . Wait, same thing.

If you're not in a hurry to go somewhere, just be mindful that those behind you may want to get where they're going sometime today.

UNWRITTEN RULE #27: One should always turn right on red when allowed to do so.

SIDEWALK. SIDERUN. SAME DIFFERENCE.

Why do they call it rush hour when nothing moves?
—ROBIN WILLIAMS

You've probably forgotten that there are three types of irony, so we'll give you a quick example of "situational irony." That's the type that occurs when you get the opposite result of what you expect.

You've taken up jogging because you realize you're a fat, lazy slob, and you'd like to live past forty-five. However, your poor decision-making has continued. You run *right down the middle of the street* instead of, say, on the sidewalk or on the shoulder. A distracted driver, who is not following the "no texting while driving" rule runs over you, and suddenly you're a greasy spot on the street. The irony is that what you did for your health killed you.

You should not be running in the middle of a traffic lane just because it's early in the morning. Cars still use the street, even before 6 A.M. Get off the road! Or at least get on the shoulder! Pretend you have a basic grasp of the concept of self-preservation.

UNWRITTEN RULE #28: One should never jog in the middle of a street.

ORDER FOR ONE

The drive-through at fast food places is designed for those in a hurry who are grabbing a quick bite before heading to work. Very little (that isn't actually life-threatening) in life is more annoying than sitting behind some civility-lacking, mouth-breathing doofus who is ordering a repast for seven co-workers, all of whom have special orders.

Earth to doofus: Get out of the damn car. Go into the damn restaurant. Get out your damn little pieces of paper with separate orders and your damn separate piles of money, and order the damn food at the counter! Yes, you'll still irritate those in line behind you, but you won't be as likely to cause a road-rage—or drive-through-lane-rage—incident.

UNWRITTEN RULE #29: One should never make large, complicated orders at the drive-through window of a fast food restaurant.

ATM FURY

Men can read maps better than women 'cause only the male mind could conceive of one inch equaling a hundred miles.
—ROSEANNE BARR

You're in a hurry. You need a few bucks. You get up to the ATM, and—oh, thank you, dear Jesus—there's only one guy in front of you. You'll get through this in a jiff . . . but, wait!

First, the guy has to fish out his wallet. Then, he's got to fill in a deposit slip. Only then does he actually put his card into the machine. You wait. The doofus has multiple transactions. You feel your ears turning red. You turn on the radio, in an attempt to lower your blood pressure. You start thinking about baseball and dead relatives . . . the same stuff you do to avoid premature ejaculation.

Finally! He seems to be done. His card pops out. You get ready to pull ahead . . . and *no freaking way*. The guy spends another minute organizing all his crap before pulling away from the machine. That is the unpardonable sin of his transaction. All he has to do is pull up a few feet, get out of your way, and *then* get his stuff together. If you could push a button that would cause him and his car to drop into an alligator-filled lake, you know you'd do it.

UNWRITTEN RULE #30: One should always be prepared at the drive-up ATM, and one should pull away from the ATM before organizing one's wallet and receipts.

I TAKE CARE OF MY KIDS (EXCEPT WHEN THEY PISS ME OFF)

You've got your kids buckled into the seat belts and booster seats. Good for you, law-abiding citizen! Kudos! Clearly, you care about your children's safety. Or do you?

When your kids begin screaming at each other, which they will inevitably do as boredom creeps in, then you are *not* protecting them by turning around, taking your eyes off the road, and attempting to discipline them en route to the Stop & Shop.

This precise situatation is why God invented such things as portable DVD players and video games. Give your children this juvenile version of crack, and they won't be as likely to get bored. As a result, they'll be less likely to say "Mom! Bobby touched me!" And you won't have to take your eyes off the road in order to discipline your kids while speeding.

UNWRITTEN RULE #31: One should never take one's eyes off the road in order to turn around and threaten children who are misbehaving in the back seat of one's car.

AUTOMOBILE, THY NAME IS VANITY

We're not against vanity plates per se. Sure, they usually indicate that the driver is a flaming douche, but they also can reflect pride in one's alma mater (GOHEELZ, for UNC-Chapel Hill fans), one's family (5KIDZ!), or one's faith (GODRULZ).

Our problem with those plates is that most of them make absolutely no sense except to the driver and his family (if he has one) or friends (which he probably *doesn't* have). The riddles these hieroglyphics create can become the visual equivalent of "ear worms" (you can't focus on your meeting because you're still trying to figure out what ZSPLAT means). They can even cause accidents (you're so focused on the plate that you rear end the guy in front of you).

If you have so much expendable income that you can throw away sixty bucks on special plates, please share that largesse with us, D-BAG.

UNWRITTEN RULE #32: One should avoid vanity license plates that make no sense to the general public.

FLYING DAGGERS ARE EVIL

It has snowed a (technical term) shitload. Your car is buried under feet of the white stuff like some sort of gas-guzzling igloo. Nonetheless, you don't have one of those cushy government jobs that give you a day off or an "optional" workday during blizzard conditions. You've got to get to work, and you'd better be on time because the boss always makes a point of being the first one to the office regardless of the weather.

We understand you're in a hurry, and we understand that shoveling snow off one's car is a sucky, thankless task. Be that as it may, please finish the task. By that, we mean don't just scrape the snow and ice off the front and rear windshields. Take a moment or two extra and get the drifts off the top of your car as well.

Why? Well, picture this. You're driving (too fast for the conditions, a-hole) to work when, like the ice shelf cracking in the global-warming sun, a giant chunk of snow and ice flies off your car and heads straight for the vehicle (driving too close for the conditions, a-hole) behind you.

The result could be serious injury to the driver or (worse, much worse) a lawsuit that takes what little you have. At a good clip, flying snow and ice is bad news. Don't be that guy (actually, others will call you "that a-hole") whose car becomes a weapon of mass destruction.

UNWRITTEN RULE #33: One should always remove *all* snow and ice from one's car before getting out on the road.

FLAMING MISSILES ARE BAD

Every time I see an adult on a bicycle, I no longer despair for the future of the human race.

—H. G. WELLS

First of all, we're shocked that some people still smoke. Most cars these days don't have "cigarette lighters"; they have tiny electrical outlets one can use to charge various electronic devices. Ashtrays have been replaced by cup holders. Most people appear to have gotten the message: Smoking is bad, mkay?

Some folks, however, continue to live in the 1950s. At that time, smoking made men more macho and women more alluring. Doctors smoked in hospitals while talking to patients about their chances of overcoming cancer (nil). No one knew what the hell a "surgeon general" was.

Smokers today not only have death wishes, but they also lack common decency in many cases. How do we know? Because we have had burning objects hurled toward us from passing automobiles. Goddamn, is that rude!

It's also potentially dangerous. You may have sucked out all the carcinogens in your cancer stick, but the damn thing is *still lit*. After the flaming missile has bounced off the front of our car, it could then go into the median and start a fire.

If you want to kill yourself via coffin nails, that's fine with us. There'll be one fewer idiot in the world. But please leave us out of your death-wishing plans.

UNWRITTEN RULE #34: One should never throw a lit cigarette out of a car.

THE ROAD IS NOT A GARBAGE DUMP

Although they won't cause fires like cigarettes, people who throw trash out of their cars are even lower on the evolutionary scale. If you look at diagrams of protozoa or one-celled amoeba or whatever those things are called that have just crawled out of the sea and onto dry land, you'll notice that behind them, still mostly submerged, are trash-flingers.

We're not even sure what "reasoning" governs this destructive act. Do you have such a phobia about cleanliness in your own car that you have no problem polluting the planet instead? Are you afraid of germs that might breed in those uneaten bites of coneys and tots? Most likely you're just lazy and thoughtless.

Please stop treating Earth as a giant landfill. Save your stuff until you get to a place where you can dispose of it—or better yet, recycle it—properly. Otherwise, your immortal soul will rot in hell until all the Styrofoam containers you've thrown out have disintegrated. Hope you bring plenty of sunscreen to the hereafter! Styrofoam takes more than a million years to decompose.

UNWRITTEN RULE #35: One should never, ever, *ever* throw trash out of one's car.

DON'T REVEAL YOUR (RED) RUBBERNECK

We're not blaming movies, television, video games, or any other form of media for violence, but it has desensitized us to an alarming degree. Case in point: Folks slow down and rubberneck like crazy when there's a bad crash on the side of the road.

Some drivers might be slowing down in order to be safe, but the majority of them (we believe) just want to see some real-life carnage. They're hoping for stray limbs or, at the very least, pints of spilled blood. They cluck their tongues and act sympathetic, but really, they're just entertaining mild blood lust.

Not only is it karmically icky to receive titillation from someone else's misfortune, it can become (thanks, John Lennon) Instant Karma if you take your eyes off the road long enough. You see, when you're not looking at the road, you're likely to hit someone or something. Then, it may be your blazing automobile people are slowing down to stare at and photograph with their cell phones. Enjoy your fifteen minutes! It may be all the time you've got left!

UNWRITTEN RULE #36: One should never "rubberneck" while on the road.

IRONICALLY, YOU'RE NOT VERY BRIGHT

A city that outdistances man's walking powers is a trap for man.
—ARNOLD TOYNBEE, HISTORIAN

At first, we try to be charitable and assume that you simply have forgotten to turn off your brights when approaching us. Because we've seen movies suggesting that flashing our brights at you could draw us into a gory death (something to do with gang initiation or some such crap; probably not true, but why take chances?), we choose not to send you the universal, "Put on your dims, dickweed," symbol.

We can't help noticing, though, that another driver has "flashed" you, and you respond by...doing nothing. You keep your brights on because the only motorist you care about is yourself. We once could see, but now we're blind, and we think you're amazingly graceless.

Yes, it's a pain to keep clicking your brights on and off. Nonetheless, it's a must. If you blind us, we could have an accident. If that has no impact on you, then keep in mind we could impact you at sixty-five (or more) miles an hour because we are blinded temporarily. Don't be a douche, okay?

UNWRITTEN RULE #37: One should never drive with one's brights on when other cars approach.

HONK IF YOU'RE A D-BAG!

The light changes to green, and before you even can put your foot on the gas pedal, some NASCAR-loving, mouth-breathing cousin to a platypus is honking his (got to be a "he") horn at you. At this moment, you wish you could shoot death rays out of your car's exhaust pipe and remove this crude, graceless excuse for a human being from the face of the Earth and do yourself and all fellow Earthlings a favor.

If you are *that guy*, what is your major malfunction? Sure, if we were sitting there for a few seconds, clearly texting or yelling at our kids or doing something other than paying attention to driving, then a "friendly" tap on your horn might be warranted. But you didn't even give us a chance to react.

Since we can't shoot death rays, we'll have to settle for the next best thing and sit at the light—purposefully this time—for a few extra beats, just to, you know, make you aware of your douche-bag-iness. On second thought, we'll ignore your affront and just drive on. We'll be the adults on the road. Besides, with a hair-trigger temper like yours, any response from us could lead to a road-rage incident.

UNWRITTEN RULE #38: One should never honk at another motorist just because he or she does not begin moving at the exact second the light changes to green.

YOU'RE A PARASITE

You're driving down the street, obeying all traffic and safety rules. All's cool with your world. Suddenly, you hear the sound of a siren. Being a conscientious person (unlike all these goddamn jerks on the road), you slow down, get in the right lane, and wait for the fire engine to pass. That's when your a-hole detector goes off.

Just behind the speeding emergency vehicle, on its way to a burning building or fiery crash, is some random motorist using the fire engine's rapid pace as an opportunity to speed. In other words, the driver is acting like a parasite, serving no useful purpose, yet stuck to the emergency vehicle like a piglet on a juicy teat.

Are you kidding me? Some random jerk-off is using other people's misfortune as an excuse to speed and (most likely) get away with it? That's just low, lower than a snake's belly, lower than his (got to be a "he") mama's mammaries.

The proper procedure is to *stay away* from the speeding police car, ambulance, or fire engine, not to use it as a chance to get to a strip club a couple minutes quicker.

UNWRITTEN RULE #39: One should never follow closely behind a speeding emergency vehicle.

ENTRANCE RAMP.
ENTRANCE RAMP. GET IT?!?

**The longest journey begins with a single step,
not with a turn of the ignition key.**

—EDWARD ABBEY, AUTHOR

We've already written the riot act for those who like to "slalom" in traffic (see Rule #17). Those folks are bad enough. Even worse, however, are those who don't even have the courtesy to slalom in legitimate lanes.

Let us, for a moment, focus on the particular species *Douchebagus zoomdweebie*. This guy (almost certain to be a guy) is in such a big hurry that he'll slalom into an entrance ramp in order to pass a few other motorists. Why is he in such a hurry? Because, dumbass, he's more important than you. Just ask him!

Yep, he's not content with going from left lane to right lane to middle lane to right lane to left lane. He's using a nonexistent lane as well, whenever it happens not to have any drivers in it. He'll zoom over, and just before he should be exiting the interstate, *surprise*, he's back in your lane, missing you by inches.

Look, we realize he's white trash or a stupid teenager or—most likely—a stupid, white trash (redundant, we know) teen. But you shouldn't honk or provoke him. He's crazy. Let him be the idiot. You just get on with your life.

UNWRITTEN RULE #40: One should never use an entrance ramp to "slalom" around other motorists.

CHAPTER 2

UNWRITTEN RULES

IN THE WORKPLACE

Work sucks. It's mind-numbing, soul-sucking, and filled with three piece suit–wearing piranha. Of course, some people (claim to) love their jobs, but even most of *them* have a stray complaint or two because— apologies to Pat Benetar—work, not love, is life's true battlefield.

Skirmishes over doughnuts! Donnybrooks over deadlines! Fisticuffs over idea thievery! And the list goes on and on . . .

Since work typically does suck, we believe it should not be made worse by the complete absence of collegiality. Therefore, we offer advice on how to avoid uncouth etiquette at work. Let the boss be a douche. All you underlings should be kind to each other.

DON'T BOGART THAT LAST DOUGHNUT, MY FRIEND

Point me out the happy man and I will point you out either egotism, selfishness, evil—or else an absolute ignorance.
—GRAHAM GREENE

Someone brought doughnuts! Isn't that sweet! Now *that* is a person who understands the concept of civility, courtesy, and empty calories! You can't get to the box right away because your boss is yapping away about how you didn't send the report to Kalamazoo in a timely fashion.

Finally, he docks you for a half-day's pay and leaves you alone. You rush over to the box and . . . NOOOOOO! Some jerk has eaten the last doughnut. Talk about insult to injury! First, your boss rips you a new one, and then you can't satisfy your jones for artery-clogging breakfast treats.

If there's one doughnut left, don't take it unless you've polled others first. If you're the guy who takes the last doughnut, others will know, and you will get a worse reputation even than that suck-up in cubicle five.

UNWRITTEN RULE #41: One should never take the last doughnut in the box.

PERSONAL SPACE IS A GOOD THING, A VERY GOOD THING

Most people are aware of personal space, that unspoken zone one should place between oneself and another. Some people, however, were born lacking the personal space gene. Personally, we feel that telethons should be devoted to these unfortunate souls who don't understand the discomfort they inflict on others by getting right up in their grill.

If you find people surreptitiously backing away from you or fixing their faces in unpleasant expressions at your appearance, then you may be one of these personal space invaders. If so, here's a quick rule of thumb: You should remain at least an arm's length away from someone else, unless you are on intimate terms with him or her. Also, gentlemen, while you personally may be "cool" with man hugs, most men are not. Please keep your hands—and huggy arms—to yourselves.

UNWRITTEN RULE #42: One should never invade the personal space of others.

INAPPROPRIATE E-MAILS AREN'T US

Inappropriate e-mails take many forms: dirty jokes, chain letters, cartoons that make fun of various religions, cutesy pictures of one's family that cause others to exceed the limits of their e-mail storage, politically slanted "humor," requests for sexual favors from comely fellow employees, threats against colleagues, photos of one's genitalia (unless you're Brett Favre).

Picture your mother, someone else's mother, God, Jesus, Buddha, Vishnu, or a mean nun as you think about sending or forwarding that e-mail. If you wouldn't want one of the people/beings/mean nuns on that list to receive your e-mail, then you shouldn't send it.

UNWRITTEN RULE #43: One should never send an e-mail at work that others might consider inappropriate.

DECORATE WITH DECORUM

It is human to want to be unique, especially when one works at a soul-sucking job inside an impersonal cubicle tabulating figures and begging for death. Nonetheless, one should be careful with one's efforts to personalize one's cubicle or workspace.

Pictures featuring nakedness of any kind, including that of one's adorable children . . . uh, that's a no. Cute animal posters with slogans like "Hang in there!!!!" Puh-lease. When in doubt about the appropriateness of your decor, you might consult a colleague. Make sure it's a trusted colleague; otherwise, someone may give you bad advice because he did not read Rule #53 about backstabbers.

Remember: You're at work. For God's sake, be tasteful, or at least pretend to have some taste.

UNWRITTEN RULE #44: One should always decorate one's workspace or cubicle appropriately.

STOP ASKING QUESTIONS

The best way to appreciate your job is to imagine yourself without one.
—OSCAR WILDE

Meetings can be an important way for colleagues to share information, brainstorm ideas, and streamline processes. They also can be soul-sucking wastes of time, and anything that makes them feel even more interminable is not welcome.

Nonetheless, some people do not seem to understand this. When the boss finally shuts up and asks, "Are there any questions?" they *actually start to ask questions.* Don't they know that they're *not* supposed to ask anything because everyone else wants to get the heck out of Dodge?

Oh, wait. That's right. They're asking questions because they're brown-nosing goofballs. Just so they can score a few points with the boss, they keep the meeting lasting just a bit longer. Earth to you, brown-nosing goofball: Everyone wishes you would drop dead.

UNWRITTEN RULE #45: One should never ask questions after an interminable meeting when the boss asks, "Are there any questions?"

WHO PUT THIS GUY IN CHARGE?

Your boss is gone when it's time for the daily office meeting, and you're psyched that—just this once—you won't have to sit through all the boring claptrap. You actually can get something done instead.

Then, what the . . . That suck-up—what's his name? Bob? Bill? Dick? Must be Dick—comes by your cubicle and lets you know the meeting will take place after all, with *him* in charge.

You slink off to the meeting, kissing goodbye all that dreamed-of productivity. The meeting drags on, with that dorky suck-up putting everyone through his or her paces, acting like he's the boss. Everyone at the table wonders the same thing: Why would the boss put *this* a-hole in charge?

Later on, you make a horrifying discovery. Dick took it upon himself to "take over" for the boss. The boss never asked Dick to lead the meeting. Stunned, you and your colleagues ponder the best course of action: voodoo doll? Or forward him a computer virus? Ah, the heck with it. Just keep bad-mouthing him behind his back the way you've always done.

UNWRITTEN RULE #46: One should never pretend to be the boss when the boss is absent unless the boss actually has put one in charge.

PEOPLE HATE SUCK-UPS

You learn that your boss attended the University of Tennessee and, as they say there, "bleeds orange." Slowly, but surely, you decorate your cubicle with orange and white Tennessee Volunteers pennants and stickers. Congratulations! You're a suck-up, and everybody hates you!

Of course you should treat your boss with respect. That goes without saying. However, there's a fine line between showing respect and puckering up to the supervisor's posterior. Stay on this side of the line, and you're a competent employee. Cross that line, and you're a sub-human leech.

UNWRITTEN RULE #47: One should never suck up to the boss in order to curry favor.

COMMUNICATE!

Oh, you hate your job? Why didn't you say so? There's a support group for that. It's called everybody, and they meet at the bar.
—DREW CAREY

Businesses, even those devoted to communication, often have pitiful intraoffice communication that can lead to vicious squabbles. One department comes up with a new idea, doesn't share it, and then gets its collective feathers bent when another department comes up with a similar idea and does share it, thus getting kudos, and possibly, bonuses.

Even within departments, communication breakdowns are rampant and cause those working cheek to jowl to hiss and wail at one another.

Rumors are rife everywhere. Bitching, moaning, and complaining about one's job and one's coworkers—and coming up with colorful stories to assuage boredom—is rampant. The situation is only made worse when people simmer in silence, assuming rumors to be true.

UNWRITTEN RULE #48: Colleagues should always communicate with one another and should never make assumptions.

DON'T TALK IN THE DOORWAY

Doorways, the bottoms/tops of staircases or escalators, and the entrances to elevators are designed for one thing: movement. They are passageways, which means they are intended for people to pass (quickly) through them.

Nonetheless, folks often use these passageways to yak, gossip, chew the fat, and have verbal intercourse. Why do they do this?!? Aren't their cubicles big enough? Won't they see Bob from accounting in the lunchroom in a couple of hours? Have they overrun their texting allotments? What is so damn important that it causes them to freeze in midstream, inconveniencing folks who just want to leave/enter the room/elevator/staircase?

UNWRITTEN RULE #49: One should always remember that doorways, staircases, and elevator entrances are inappropriate spots to stop and chitchat.

DEAD WOOD IS FOR THE FOREST FLOOR

Every department has at least one person who seems to collect a paycheck for doing absolutely nothing at all, and what's worse, the boss often seems to *know* this employee is dead wood, yet she refuses to go after him with a chainsaw.

Perhaps he has "dirt" on the boss. Perhaps he's the nephew of the company's founder. Perhaps the one thing he's good at is being a sycophant. Perhaps the boss is just a spineless coward who's afraid to make waves in the office.

If you are this dead wood, then we've got some advice: Grow up. Do your freaking job. Stop making everyone else take up the slack for your lazy butt. Stop being a worthless drain.

UNWRITTEN RULE #50: One should always work hard at one's job and never be "dead wood" in the office.

GOD HATES IDEA THIEVES

All paid jobs absorb and degrade the mind.
—ARISTOTLE

Bob, the new guy in accounts receivable, comes up with a way to streamline the widgets process . . . or whatever it is folks do in Accounts Receivable. His immediate supervisor, Dick, praises Bob for his ingenuity. Bob expects a raise or at least a pat on the back from the big boss.

Instead, Dick goes to the big boss with "his" new idea about how to streamline the widgets process. Dick heads for a promotion. And Bob? Bob remains the new guy in accounts receivable, harboring a hatred for Dick that eventually will lead Bob to commit an act of workplace violence.

Ideas belong to those who suggest them, not to backstabbing supervisors. Let people have their credit if they've earned it.

UNWRITTEN RULE #51: One should never steal another's idea and claim it as his or her own.

BE A TEAM PLAYER

You hated it in school, and you hate it even more at work. You know what we're talking about. You're part of a "team" that has to prepare a huge, involved report, yet you seem to be the only member of the "team" who's even attempting to carry the weight.

Or worse. You're that coarse, uncouth Neanderthal who sits by while others do your share of the work because you know they're too nice to say anything. Well, maybe they are, but *we're* not. You're a coarse, uncouth Neanderthal. Your family tree has no branches. Your children hate you and are going to grow up to become drug addicts (if they're not already doing lines in the family room). You give white trash a bad name.

UNWRITTEN RULE #52: When one is named a team player, one should always, in fact, *be* a team player.

THE BACKSTABBERS

Unfortunately, Julius Caesar isn't the last example of a person whose colleagues stab him in the back. At least, these days, words have replaced knives (at least we hope they have, for your sake).

If you backstab, then you are lower on the food chain than a banana slug: You smile and act friendly toward a colleague, only to write memos to your boss about his or her egregious errors, stale breath, generally terrible work ethic, etc.

You want to get ahead. We understand. But the way to do that is to rise above others with your performance, not by making like it's the Ides of March.

UNWRITTEN RULE #53: One should never stab colleagues in the back in order to progress one's own career (or for any other reason, either).

BACK *AWAY* FROM THE BUTTON!

Do you see the way the "up" button is illuminated? That means the button has been pressed. Did you happen to notice that we're in a high-rise building possessing many floors? Perhaps you might also have noticed the limited number of available elevators.

In a tactful way, we're trying to call you an insensitive idiot for pushing the damn button every few seconds. All of us are annoyed at waiting, but we were raised properly and understand the basic laws of elevators and physics that guide how quickly a car will arrive.

When you keep jamming the button, you just remind the rest of us of our plight—stuck in office lobby limbo awaiting a swift ride to the soul-sucking job we would have laughed at in high school. Thanks a lot, man.

UNWRITTEN RULE #54: One should only push the elevator button one time.

NOT IN THE ELEVATOR, MAN!

If you can do a half-assed job of anything,
you're a one-eyed man in a kingdom of the blind.
—KURT VONNEGUT

The Irish have a saying: 'Tis better to let it out and bear the shame than keep it in and bear the pain. In other words, when you've got to pass gas, then you'd better follow nature's dictum.

But not in the elevator, man!

We're trapped now, with the castoffs of your el grande burrito and cheap beer that's never made any town famous. Couldn't you have left that outside the elevator or just waited until you got to your floor?

Now, not only are we confined to a car with noxious fumes, but we're all looking for the culprit and mortified at the thought that someone will think we are the ones who let fly.

**UNWRITTEN RULE #55: One should
never pass gas in an elevator.**

APPOINTMENT TIMES ARE NOT "SUGGESTIONS"

The appointment was for 1:00 P.M., and it's already 1:35 P.M. You've received neither call nor text to inform you of a change in your prospective client's plans. Now, you face a dilemma. Should you leave and reschedule? What if the client decides to take her business elsewhere?

Should you call? If so, how do you avoid coming off as whiny? And worst of all: What if this waiting game interferes with the appointment you've made for 3:00 P.M.?

No one should be put in this situation. People who believe "fashionably late" extends beyond parties to business engagements are uncouth, coarse, ill-mannered trailer trash gussied up by Prada or Armani.

Everyone's time is precious, not just yours. You are not proving how "important" you are by making others wait on your dilatory ass. All you're proving is that you think etiquette is a four-letter word.

UNWRITTEN RULE #56: One should always keep appointments. Should plans be forcibly changed, one should always communicate changes to those who are waiting on one.

IF YOU DON'T LIKE YOUR JOB, THEN QUIT!

It's just a job. Grass grows, birds fly, waves pound the sand. I beat people up.

—MUHAMMAD ALI

You hate your job. Cool. After all, you work retail, with its "customer is always right" crap. We wouldn't want to be in your position either. But here's the thing . . . We don't want to hear about how much you hate your job.

Sure, the guy in line before us was a douche with no manners who treated you like you're less than human. That's not right. Nonetheless, if you *ever* want to go beyond retail or, perhaps, make it to retail management, then you've got to save your spleen and vent it in the break room.

Other customers, who are *not* douches, do not need to hear the bitter comments your make to your coworkers about other (douche-like) customers, the fact that you're not getting your break on time, or the way other coworkers suck at their jobs.

That's just unprofessional and rude. If you hate your job so much, then get another one! If you can't, then do your best at the one you've got. It's not *our* fault you chose to drop out of high school.

UNWRITTEN RULE #57: One should never make complaints about one's retail job in front of customers.

KEEP THOSE VOICEMAILS SHORT

Beep. "Uh, yeah, Bob? This is Dan. You know those reports I left on your desk? Well, you need to make sure you get the Rogers and Poole ones done by Friday, but I need the Taylor and Branch ones completed by Wednesday. Oh, no, wait. It's the Branch and Poole ones I need by Wednesday. You don't need to turn in the Rogers and Taylor reports until Friday. Actually, the Branch one I really need ASAP, so if you can get it done any earlier, make it your top priority, then that would be great. I'll be out of the office for most of the rest of this week, just so you know. Oh, yeah. I meant to put a sticky note on the Branch file concerning tax information, so don't forget to look up tax information in regard to the Branch file going back, say, five years. If you absolutely do need to reach me, then you can reach me at 232-444-5198." *Beep.*

Are you kidding? The number is not until the very end. It's only said once, so if you didn't catch it the first time, you have to listen to this *entire* freaking message again in order to get those digits. But that's okay because you'll have to listen to this Tolstoy-length voicemail several times just to get straight all of the stuff that you need to do, and you know you'd better get it done correctly, or you'll probably get fired.

Dan, you're a thoughtless jerk of a boss. Don't be so lazy. Write down instructions next time.

UNWRITTEN RULE #58: One should keep the length of voicemails to a minimum and offer one's call back number at least twice.

ISN'T THAT AGAINST COMPANY POLICY?

When you start a new job, one of the first things you're handed is a company handbook. Then, you're asked to familiarize yourself with its every nook and cranny. As a courteous, hard-working employee, you do just that.

A few weeks—hell, probably a few hours—into your new job, you find that people routinely ignore tenets of the handbook that are emphasized repeatedly. At first, you think it's just lazy, shiftless employees who are guilty of ignoring company policy. You continue to do the right thing, as per the handbook.

Then, one day, your boss chews you out because you didn't complete a task in a timely manner. But, you protest, it takes a little while to do this since I'm following the handbook's procedures. Your boss looks at you like you're dumber than razor-wire scuba gear. "Just get it done. *Now*," she says.

Instead of being a hero, on the fast track to success, because of your compliance with company values, you're considered a none-too-bright dilatory jerk-off. You've realized too late that the stupid handbook is just a legal formality, designed to be ignored or obsolete upon printing.

UNWRITTEN RULE #59: Companies that claim to have company policies should, in fact, follow those company policies.

DESTRUCTIVE CRITICISM IS SOUL-SUCKING AND RUDE

*It's a recession when you neighbor loses his job;
it's a depression when you lose yours.*
—HARRY S. TRUMAN

Everyone makes mistakes. In addition, people often *think* they're doing something correctly, only to find the boss expected something totally different. That's sort of an *ex-post-facto* mistake.

If an employee screws up something, then, yes, he or she should be taken to task for it, but bosses who choose to focus solely on destructive criticism are dictatorial little Hitlers who should stop being head of accounting and should, instead, be whisked away to an island nation where they can play at fascism all day long in the sun and surf.

Focusing solely on someone's mistake leaves no room for solutions. It browbeats employees, makes them resentful, and causes them to hate their jobs. Sure, some employees are awful and should be let go, but adopting a scorched-earth policy for every misstep will alienate valuable workers as well.

Next time, just acknowledge the mistake, let the employee offer possible solutions to the mistake, and end by praising the employee for making the best of a bad situation.

UNWRITTEN RULE #60: One should always use constructive, not destructive, criticism.

YOU'RE SUCH A GREAT WORKER! HERE'S MORE WORK!

Hard workers, and those willing to volunteer to help out, often find themselves taken advantage of. For example, Sylvia is always the first person to arrive at the office in the morning, so the boss has gotten in the habit of saving "suck work" for her to complete before everyone else starts straggling in. Bob, who's always willing to help out, starts being overloaded with extra assignments, and, of course, Bob is too nice to say "no."

People should not be punished for having strong work ethics and/ or high-caliber collegiality skills. These employees should be rewarded for their efforts. If money isn't available for bonuses, then give them a free day off or at least allow them to leave earlier than everyone else now and again.

Better yet, start giving that sucky work to employees who routinely come in late, who have rotten attitudes, and who make your life more difficult. Give those extra assignments to employees you would like to see quit.

UNWRITTEN RULE #61: Employers should not "reward" good employees with extra, lousy work that should be given to people who are *not* good employees.

DON'T LEAVE ME GUESSING

It's your day off! Hooray! In fact, you're facing a couple of days before you have to put your nose back to the grindstone (or back up your boss's posterior). Your phone rings. You look at the display. Crap. It's work. You decide not to answer, expecting your boss to leave a message.

After some time, it becomes clear that the thoughtless bastard isn't going to leave a message. Your blood pressure starts to tick up. Should you call him back? Are you going to lose your job if you don't? Hell, is *that* why he's calling? You know you screwed up on the McLaughlin report, but, overall, your record is pretty good.

Right about the time you start to relax again (martini number three or four), he calls back. Once again, he leaves no message. If you call, you're sure he's going to force you to come into work on one or both of your days off. At least you think that's what it is. OMG! What does he want?!? You start to feel like a character in a Poe story, obsessed to the point of madness.

UNWRITTEN RULE #62: A boss should always leave a message when calling an employee on his or her day off.

YOUR TIME-MANAGEMENT SKILLS SUCK!

*It's not the most intellectual job in the world,
but I do have to know the letters.*

—VANNA WHITE

If you always find yourself stressing over deadlines, unable to eat, wishing you could just die and get it over with, then we have news for you: Your time-management skills suck!

If you have rotten time-management skills, then you will hate your job, will not succeed at your job, and, quite likely, will be fired from your job. In addition, you'll give yourself ulcers, be mean to your children, and be unable to enjoy sexual intercourse.

Jeez, all of this because you don't know how to pace yourself? Sounds pretty stupid to us.

Look, there's no big secret. Think of work as a big candy bar, one of those that breaks apart into pre-cut pieces. Just take a piece or two each day, rather than trying to cram the whole thing in your mouth at the last minute. Don't give yourself any downtime until you're finished with a task.

As long as you're doing something that moves you in the right direction, then, well, you're moving in the right direction. Try it! Enjoy your life again! Stop beating your kids! Stop experiencing frigidity/impotence in the bedroom! Stop acting like you're not responsible for the situation!

UNWRITTEN RULE #63: One should work hard to develop effective time-management skills.

WHISTLE WHILE YOU WORK . . . NOT!

Walt Disney should be thawed out of his cryogenic holding tank and kicked wantonly for helping perpetuate the "cheery" concept that it's totally cool to whistle while one works.

This is true *only if* you're a princess surrounded by seven dwarves (Disney called them dwarfs, which was the correct plural then), but it's not accurate for desk jockeys. Your colleagues will (or certainly will want to) find a large club, bat, bludgeon, paperweight, knick-knack, or dwarf-sized coworker and beat you over the head with it if they have to hear *one more goddamn time* your off-key whistling rendition of "Single Ladies (Put a Ring on It)" or (during Yuletide) "Last Christmas."

Perhaps whistling or singing keeps *you* from going insane, but it does not have the same effect on your coworkers. Save your self-imagined talents for the shower or car.

UNWRITTEN RULE #64: One should never sing or whistle at work, despite Walt Disney's suggestion to the contrary.

ADVICE IGNORERS

"I'm really having a tough time with the boss. We keep bumping heads. What should I do?"

"Well, she's not an ogre. I think if you just send an e-mail, asking for a meeting with her, then go in and talk honestly about the situation, then that will help."

"Hey, thanks! I really appreciate your advice!"

Then the SOB completely ignores your advice. In fact, you can hear him a few minutes/hours/seconds later asking another cubicle colleague the same question. Three words pop into your head: "What a douche."

People who seek advice only to ignore it must have serious psychological problems. Perhaps they're just hoping the advice *you* give will be the same advice they get from the voices in their heads. Most likely, they lack self-confidence and want to be able to blame someone else if things turn out badly.

If you're one of these advice ignorers, then you should change your pitch a bit. Tell your colleague about your situation and admit that you're asking a lot of people about it because you aren't sure what to do. Then you spark a friendly competition among your colleagues—Whose advice will Dick pick?—instead of sowing the seeds of discord.

UNWRITTEN RULE #65: One should never implore a colleague for advice on a thorny matter only to ignore that advice without comment.

YO, RINGO, STOP THE BEAT!

**Monday morning. Time to pay for your two days
of debauchery, you hungover drones.**

—MONTGOMERY BURNS (THE SIMPSONS)

We're not sure what's worse. Is it people who sing or whistle off-key during work hours, or is it people who drum a constant tattoo on their desks. Sometimes, they use pens. Sometimes, they use their fingers. Always, they bug the living bejesus out of us.

Perhaps it's a nervous habit, and you're not even aware that you're channeling Lars Ulrich while we're on the phone trying to get a prospect to sign with us. We'll just try to ignore that constant TAP, TAP, TAP, TAP, TAP, TAP, TAP, TAP, TAP, TAP.

Oh, who are we kidding? Stop doing that now before we take that pen and shove it into your eye socket!

UNWRITTEN RULE #66: One should never make annoying tapping noises during work hours.

IF YOU BORROW, RETURN

First, it's your stapler. Then, it's your box of paper clips. Next, it's your scissors. It's like everything in the office is sucking into a black hole of much-needed office supplies. You do a little investigating, and . . . oh. Turns out the "black hole" is Barb in accounting, who likes to "borrow" people's stuff, but "forgets" to return it.

Well, Barb from accounting, we've got news for you: Borrowing without returning is better known as *stealing*. You're not public enemy number one—yet—but you are office enemy number one (well, maybe number three, after the boss and that copy-machine hogging douche bag who brays loudly at his own unfunny jokes).

If someone isn't around, then it's okay to borrow her stapler or scissors for a moment . . . as long as you return them. After the objects have suited your needs, they're still going to be needed by their original owners.

UNWRITTEN RULE #67: One should always return ASAP any object borrowed from a colleague.

PUT THE DAMN THING ON VIBRATE!

The reason you tend to leave your cell phone on your desk when you go to meetings or take a break is because it's constantly jingling, letting you know you have a new text. Well, guess what, dipwad? We can hear that constant tintinnabulation as well, and it's about to get on our last nerve.

It's even worse when you actually have the thing with you in meetings. It dings and dongs because, unlike you, it seems to have a job to do. You're supposed to be helping your colleagues figure out copy for the new bidet account. You're *not* supposed to be a slave to that stupid bell, and we certainly don't want to be slaves to it either. Put it on vibrate next time.

UNWRITTEN RULE #68: One should always keep one's phone on vibrate during work hours.

HELP THE IN-PERSON PERSON FIRST!

Even riddle of the sphinx-solving Oedipus wouldn't be able to figure this one out. Why do retail workers, faced with a long line of customers, answer a ringing phone . . . and then help the person on the phone instead of the three-dimensional human beings in their midst?!?

We understand that many retail workers are high schoolers, high school dropouts, folks "taking a break from college," and/or people too dumb to do much else. That's fine. All God's children need a clock to punch.

Nonetheless, we feel it imperative to point out that phones have an on-hold button while people do not. Folks too lazy to come into the store do not deserve *more* attention than those who went to the trouble to visit the store. Furthermore, if customers are standing in line, that means they're ready to *buy something*, and making sales should be your top priority.

Your manager would likely tell you that there's no crime in putting someone on hold. She would, however, tell you that losing a sale is a crime, and if you upset line-standing customers by ignoring them in favor of the phone, then you will lose sales.

UNWRITTEN RULE #69: An employee should always favor in-person customers over on-the-phone customers.

THEY HAVE IT IN FOR ME!

One of the saddest things is the only thing a man can do for eight hours a day, day after day, is work. You can't eat eight hours a day nor drink eight hours a day nor make love for eight hours— all you can do for eight hours is work, which is the reason man makes himself and everybody else so miserable and unhappy.

—WILLIAM FAULKNER

Some folks are really lucky. Nothing is ever their fault. They go through their lives, turning stuff into crap like some deadbeat King Midas, yet it's never because of them. At home? It's their spouse who causes all the problems. At work? It's their boss who is the bane of their existence. In the world at large? Good God, even total strangers have it in for them!

It's a wonder these perfect beings are able to survive at all, what with every man, woman, child, dog, pony, llama, and naked mole rat out to get them. Their lives are war zones, and everything is a potential missile.

Hey, guess what? If you believe that you are never at fault, then you are what psychologists call "delusional" and what other people call "a douche bag." It's quite possible that some people have it in for you. Backstabbers and run-of-the-mill evildoers *do* exist. However, if every single task you ever undertake goes wrong, then what is the one common denominator in that equation? Yep, that's right: *You*.

UNWRITTEN RULE #70: One should always look within and accept responsibility for one's personal failings, rather than believing others "have it in for you."

YOU'RE NOT J. EDGAR HOOVER

You aren't J. Edgar Hoover. He kept copious files on damn near everyone of any stature in the country in order to stockpile blackmail. He seems to have spent more time engaged in spying on folks who were no threat to the country than he did on going after bad guys.

Every workplace has its own Hoover, and boy, does he suck. He's the guy who'll sneak into your cubicle when you're not there and read the confidential note left by your boss on your computer. He'll riffle through your stuff to see if there's anything incriminating. His *real* job? Who cares? He thinks he's James Bond.

Work is tough enough without snoops like you around. Focus on your own job. Let the cream rise. Let folks ensnare themselves. You, my friend, are a freak.

UNWRITTEN RULE #71: One should never try to get "dirt" on coworkers or engage in spy activities at work.

LINCOLN HAWK . . . "F" OFF!

Anyone who can walk to the welfare office can walk to work.
—AL CAPP, CARTOON CHARACTER

What?! You're not familiar with the epic arm-wrestling movie, *Over the Top*, starring the great Sylvester Stallone? That's truly a shame, and ironic as well, since you seem determined to draw arm-wrestling tactics into the professional art of the handshake.

In the movie, arm wrestling promotes unity, as it helps draw together Lincoln Hawk (Stallone) and his estranged son. In this world, your hand-crushing shaking technique sows discord and makes everyone think you're an a-hole.

Yes, one should go for a firm handshake. A limp one sends the message that you are a confidence-lacking putz. On the other hand, your kung fu grip calls you out as a bully who will run ramshackle over anyone who gets in his way as he climbs to the top of the corporate ladder. Even if you are such a jerk-off, you don't really want to advertize it, do you?

A handshake should be firm but not *too* firm. It should not be an opportunity to demonstrate how much you've built up your hand muscles through frequent masturbation. Save the death grip for arm-wrestling competitions. We're pretty sure we could take you.

UNWRITTEN RULE #72: One should modulate one's handshake so that it is neither too weak nor too strong.

YOU'RE NOT MY (FACEBOOK) FRIEND ANYMORE!

We understand that, due to your lack of talent and intelligence, you've got few options available if you wish to take a step or two up the corporate ladder. Let other (suckers) people put in extra hours or come up with creative ideas, you will move ahead of them with your one marketable skill: the ability to kiss ass like no one else.

To that, um, end, you have become Facebook friends with your supervisors. Brilliant, you think. Stupid, stupid, stupid, we think.

1. One boss likes country music, so you talk about how much you like that crap. The boss above *her* loathes that schlocky shit-kicking "music" and thus thinks you're a boob. Your promotion disappears down the hillbilly highway.
2. You put an off-color joke on an *actual* friend's wall, and thus all your "friends" can see it. Your boss's "friends," even though they secretly laughed their asses off, have to feign sanctimoniousness. You get in trouble.
3. How long will it be before your "friends" start asking you to do additional grunt work for them when you're off the clock? You know, you're a buddy, right? It's not a command from your boss; it's a favor for a "friend."
4. Boss A hates Boss B, and both of them are in a secret alliance against Boss C. Now that you're "friends" with all three, you will be put into the middle of their squabbles.

UNWRITTEN RULE #73: One should not become "friends" on a social networking site with a higher-up from work.

CHAPTER 3

UNWRITTEN RULES

FOR MEN

Men are selfish. All women know this, and most men will acknowledge this character flaw as well. In fact, many wear it as a badge: Me man. Me superior. Me no care about others. But being selfish is nothing to be proud of.

Men who are manly men, *truly* men, understand that respect, courtesy, good grooming, and civility show strength. Men whose personal hygiene habits are stuck somewhere in the seventh grade may be the "bad boys" who get chicks, but they're not going to have them for very long. Men who are disrespectful to others or who constantly spoil for a fight are just bullies, and grown-ups don't take bullies seriously.

What follows is advice that can help you grow *up* already. It will teach you all that you're doing wrong in your personal life, interpersonal life, waking life, etc. and put you on the path toward maturity, adulthood, and success. Ignore these rules, and you'll die penniless, alone, and in a pool of your own filth.

IT'S CALLED A GLASS

You're not Marlon Brando, James Dean, or some other moody, troubled method actor, so here's a news flash: You do *not* look cool, sexy, interesting, intriguing, or intimidating when you pick up that carton of orange juice or milk and swig it right out of the carton.

You just look like a slobby, uncouth example of white trash ways. If that's really how you want the lady in your life (and count it miraculous if you have one of those in the first place), then keep doing it. But, perhaps, Neanderthal that you are, you're not aware of an invention that is probably lurking on a shelf of your own trailer/home/apartment/condo/cave.

It's called a "glass." Sometimes it's not really made of glass. It's plastic. But it is shaped in such a way that it holds liquid. Ask your wife/girlfriend/mother/other woman who puts up with you to show you where it's located and how to use one.

UNWRITTEN RULE #74: A gentleman should never drink directly out of a carton of milk or orange juice.

HASTA LA VISTA, DOOFUS

"What we've got here is failure to communicate." "I coulda beena contenduh." "Hasta la vista, baby." "Say hello to my leetle friend."

All right, so you've seen some quintessential guy movies. That's cool. It's even cool if, occasionally and appropriately, you slip one of these clichés into a conversation. What's definitely *not* cool is the way movie quotes constantly drool out of your mouth like pabulum.

Maybe you're misguided. Once upon a time, a girl who thought you were hot laughed at your "cleverness." She was, sad to say, delusional, and we bet that, after a while, even she wished she could put that inane movie-quoting genie back in the bottle.

We're here to do you a favor. If you ever want to get laid again, if you want to keep your friends, then by all that's holy *stop quoting films nonstop!*

UNWRITTEN RULE #75: A gentleman should quote movies sparingly, if at all.

CALL BACK

Only the wisest and stupidest of men never change.

—CONFUCIUS

Besides a scrotum, here's what it takes to be a man: Be true to your word.

Let's say you've just spent time with a fine young lady who was kind enough to invite you home. She asks you to call her, and you tell her you will. Days go by. No call. Weeks go by. No call.

Now, chances are, you were really no great shakes, and she's not, like, pining away at the lack of hearing your drunken voice on her answering machine. Nonetheless, you said you would call. Therefore, you should follow through. Isn't it time you—oh, we don't know—grew up?!?

UNWRITTEN RULE #76: A gentleman should always call back when he says that he will.

WATCH YOUR LANGUAGE

When a stupid man is doing something he is ashamed of,
he always declares that it is his duty.
—GEORGE BERNARD SHAW

You're not in the locker room anymore, son. Those days are way behind you. You're no longer a jock for whom a constant stream of profanity is as much your prop as that unused condom in your wallet. Now, you're a lower-midlevel executive in a nameless corporation with a suburban house, a wife, and 2.3 kids.

In short, it's no longer cool to cuss like a sailor. Your wife finds it threatening and abusive, and the ears on those 2.3 kids are bigger than you imagine. Now the George Washington Elementary School has *you* to thank for the "f bomb" epidemic that's hit the kindergarten wing.

Since you're a paunchy, middle-age adult, act like one. Leave the locker room behind. You were never better than third string anyway.

UNWRITTEN RULE #77: A gentleman should never curse around his children or wife/girlfriend/significant other.

PICK UP AFTER YOURSELF

Even if you have mother issues, your new girlfriend/wife/significant other is *not* your mom. She's probably got a job, just like you, and she's too busy to go around the house picking up or wiping up the snot wads, cola spills, and pieces of dead animal skin you've left to fester about your living quarters.

And those clothes! Dude. You can go to a dollar store and get a laundry basket to house them when they're dirty. You could even invest in a bureau (that's one of those squatty wooden things with the drawers you open) for your clothes when they're clean.

You're a big boy now! You don't need mommy anymore. And if just doing the right thing isn't enough, keep this in mind. If you can't become housebroken, she's going to stop putting out for you, *capiche*?

UNWRITTEN RULE #78: A gentleman always picks up after himself.

DIDN'T YOUR MOMMY TEACH YOU HOW TO DRESS YOURSELF?

*Whenever a man does a thoroughly stupid thing,
it is always from the noblest motives.*

—OSCAR WILDE

News flash: Pajama pants are not considered professional attire. Socks and sandals should never mix. Underwear should be worn *once* and then washed.

If any of this is news to you, then, clearly, the answer to the above question is "no." That's okay. We're here to help.

When you were a teenager, it was cool to look like you didn't care about your appearance. You could show up to class wearing pretty much anything that met the school's standard, and you were just fine. Nowadays, though, people laugh at you behind your back. Women might even laugh in your face. Unless you're just trying to make sure you never get laid, you need to learn how to dress.

UNWRITTEN RULE #79: A gentleman needs to dress appropriately whenever he leaves his residence.

HIT THE SHOWERS

If no one else will tell you, we will: *You stink.* Just because you're not able to get a good whiff of your pits doesn't mean all those around you aren't privy to your own special odor.

Sure, we know you have a busy nightlife and yada yada yada. We know your days are filled with exciting opportunities like playing solitaire in your cubicle or masturbating in the company washroom. Nonetheless, you *must* find time in your busy schedule to take a shower (with soap and shampoo, you understand—not just getting in the water). If you continue to smell like a sweatsock worn by a wet dog, then you will never get promoted, never be popular, and never get a woman (willingly) within ten feet of you.

UNWRITTEN RULE #80: A gentleman should shower or bathe each day.

LISTEN. *WE SAID LISTEN.*

We have two ears and one mouth so that we can listen twice as much as we speak.

—EPICTETUS

If you hear the words, "Did you hear a word I said?" far more often than the words, "Yes, let's do it right now," then you are probably one of the millions of men afflicted with willful deafness.

These poor, benighted men have a condition that blocks their ears whenever blood is diverted to their nether regions or, even worse, whenever they are confronted with information they don't want to receive.

If you are one of these unfortunate gentlemen, then it's not too late! You can actually listen. It's not too difficult. Just stop those occasional stray thoughts from reverberating through your (sex-starved) mind, look into the eyes (not the breasts) of the woman you're with, and *actually pay attention to what she says.*

In no time at all, she will feel more appreciated, and you will start getting a lot more action.

UNWRITTEN RULE #81: A gentleman should always listen carefully to a lady when she is speaking to him.

VIDEO GAMES ARE NOT REAL LIFE

We hate to tell you this, but, dude, you're not really the Master Chief fighting alongside Cortana for the fate of humanity against the Covenant. You're actually just a schmuck spending way too much time playing a video game from the Halo series.

You've become like a baby who spends hours drooling over a favorite toy or a mindless stream of videos featuring bright colors, music, and stuffed animals. In fact, that's the problem right there. Your folks didn't want to deal with taking care of you, so they had you zone out and watch "early childhood development" videos for hours on end. It's not your fault!

But you can break the cycle! You can become a denizen of our reality, a citizen of our planet. All you have to do is put down that controller and . . . get a life!

UNWRITTEN RULE #82: A gentleman should limit the time during which he plays video games.

TEASING IS NOT FLIRTING

One always has the idea of a stupid man as perfectly healthy and ordinary, and of illness as making one refined and clever and unusual.
—THOMAS MANN, AUTHOR

Some guys never learn. They would mercilessly tease the girl they liked in Ms. Saltshaker's first grade class until she (the girl *and* Ms.

Saltshaker) began to cry. Later, they would make inappropriate comments to the girl they liked in homeroom at Lazy Daze High.

Now that they are adults, they still have not figured out how to approach women in an appropriate, etiquette-friendly manner.

Teasing isn't flirting. It's just dumb. It makes you look like you're stuck in eternal adolescence, and even if you *are* stuck in eternal adolescence, you're much better off not letting her know that until she actually develops some feelings for you.

Try communicating. Try listening. Try being a genuine human being. That sounds difficult, we know, but you can do it.

UNWRITTEN RULE #83: A gentleman should know the difference between flirting and teasing.

MORNING *WOOD* = NOT GOOD

The only thing that ever consoles man for the stupid things he does is the praise he always gives himself for doing them.
—OSCAR WILDE

God clearly has a sense of humor. Case in point: Men often begin the day with engorged parts of their body saying a cheerful "Howdy!" to the world. Women, on the other hand, typically find sex first thing in the morning as palatable as a ham and Cap'n Crunch sandwich.

Morning wood is a fact of life, but using it for anything productive is probably going to remain a fantasy. Here's our advice. If you'd like the occasional morning toss in the hay, then be extremely kind and solicitous to your lover after she's awake.

In a subtle way, make your request known. Give her whatever pleasure she requests later in the day. Sooner or later, that morning wood will have it good.

UNWRITTEN RULE #84: A gentleman should never try to initiate early-morning intercourse without first laying groundwork for this activity.

MAKE PLANS? KEEP PLANS.

Men are, by nature, opportunists. Successful ones wait for opportunities and then grab onto them like a hobo attacks a Hungry Man. Often, this is a good thing. We *did* say this makes some men successful. Unfortunately, it also makes some men callous, unfeeling, self-centered clods who routinely hurt the feelings of others.

How? They are plan-breakers.

In their zest for success, they make plans with one person—often a woman—only to change those plans at the last minute, often without informing anyone of these changes. They make a date, only to get a chance to play golf with their company's executive in charge of washroom expenses. Hey, befriending *that* guy could lead to a promotion! So, so long sweetheart!

This isn't right. Integrity may not offer remuneration, but keeping it is more important than being a sycophantic flunky.

**UNWRITTEN RULE #85: One should always
keep the plans one makes.**

WOLF WHISTLING IS ONLY FOR WOLVES

Subtlety is not your strong suit. We get that. Nonetheless, whistling or
saying inappropriate things to a total stranger because she is pretty and,
possibly, dressed provocatively, is wrong. It makes you look like someone whose family tree rises—just barely—out of primordial ooze.

Most women like to be complimented for their beauty, if the compliment is offered appropriately and by someone who is not a total,
drooling stranger.

The bottom line is that if she isn't half-undressed and swinging
around on a stripper pole, then you should keep your lascivious words
and actions to yourself, and even then, you should make some effort
to comport yourself like a gentleman.

**UNWRITTEN RULE #86: A gentleman should never direct
inappropriate, lewd comments or actions toward a lady.**

PAY, YOU CHEAP BASTARD

Sure, women fought valiantly for decades to get the right to vote. In
the sixties and seventies, they worked to break through the rampant

sexism that seemed second nature to families in 1950s sitcoms. They burned bras. They fought for abortion rights. To this day, they strive to break through the glass ceiling that causes them to be paid less than men for the same work.

Yet, none of this suggests you can be a cheap, miserly, parsimonious bastard. If you're taking out a lovely lady, *especially* if you're taking her out for the first time, then you should offer to pay for the evening. If she demurs, offer again. If she still demurs, then, fine, go Dutch, or let her pay if that's how she gets her jollies.

If you think that by letting her pay you're coming off like an enlightened, equality-minded gentleman of the twenty-first century, think again. We hate to break this to you: She thinks you're cheap and, most likely, will not ever consider sleeping with you. If all you're interested in is the occasional free meal, then, by all means, just go on with your bad self.

UNWRITTEN RULE #87: A gentleman should always pay, or at least offer to pay, all expenses for dates.

DRIVE LIKE GRANNY

Macho does not prove mucho.
—ZSA ZSA GABOR

Some guys like to show that they possess testosterone by making like NASCAR drivers every time they pick up a woman for a date.

Newsflash: Ladies will not be impressed. They might associate you with NASCAR . . . fans, that is. Mouth breathers, Four Loko–guzzling, back-hair sporting troglodytes.

Drive like a mature, thoughtful adult. Better yet, drive like granny. Stop at all the yellow lights. Don't tailgate. If someone cuts you off, avoid obscene finger gestures and shouting. Save testosterone for the bedroom, and if you drive carefully, you're more likely to end up in the bedroom.

UNWRITTEN RULE #88: A gentleman should always drive carefully when escorting a date.

COMPLIMENTS REQUIRE ATTENTION TO DETAIL

The ultimate guy sin is to answer anything other than, "Are you crazy? Of course not!" to the question, "Do these jeans/Does this dress make me look fat?" A close second is not noticing when a woman has changed her appearance in some way.

You see, women already assume that men are self-centered jerks. If you fail to notice that she's gotten a haircut or styled her hair differently, or you neglect to tell her that her new top is really sexy and flattering, then you're just supporting a stereotype she already takes as gospel.

Shock her; overturn her preconceptions by noticing the things she has done to make herself look even better. You lunkhead! She's probably making the changes for you in the first place!

UNWRITTEN RULE #89: A gentleman should always notice and then compliment a woman for changes she has made to her appearance or for a new outfit.

SHUT UP ABOUT YOUR GLORY DAYS

Nothing is sadder or more pathetic than a guy who reached his peak at 17. You caught the winning pass in the 1987 Naked Mole Rats vs. Raging Platypuses game? Wow! We'll bet that earned you cheers, passage upon the shoulders of your teammates, and a hand job in the backseat of your car (possibly by your teammates, but who are we to judge).

But, dude. That was *twenty-five years ago*. No one cares about that stupid game anymore. Both team's coaches are probably dead or dribbling on themselves in a convalescent home. Your former girlfriend has gained 150 pounds and is on her fourth marriage and second stroke.

You are a guy who sells insurance, *not* the hero of a long-ago game. You're the father of two great kids, husband of a wonderful wife, and owner of a fairly nice suburban home. Your life is actually pretty damn good *right now*, so stop living in the past already! Stop annoying your coworkers, clients, and dwindling list of friends with your stories about that miraculous catch!

UNWRITTEN RULE #90: One should do one's best to leave one's glory days in the past and focus, instead, on the present.

ACCEPT SOME RESPONSIBILITY

Men are programmed to be hunters and gatherers. We're programmed to desire many sexual partners, and we seem to lack a gene allowing us to accept any responsibility when things go wrong in our lives.

Perhaps cavemen found that accepting responsibility for, say, missing the spear throw that would have netted his camp a tasty mastodon dinner led to his untimely demise. He may even have taken the mastodon's place on a spit over a primitive fire. Perhaps, during millennia of male dominance, men just got used to blaming women for their woes. The infamous King Henry VIII comes to mind.

However it happened, men are terrible at accepting responsibility. We automatically blame others (usually the women in our lives) for our woes. This trait has to change.

We don't need to accept more responsibility than we deserve for arguments and disagreements, but we need at least to accept our fair share. We can be selfish and callous, and we should just be willing to admit it from time to time.

UNWRITTEN RULE #91: A gentleman should always accept responsibility for the part he plays in arguments and disagreements.

HOLD THE INNUENDO

Don't talk about melons, tacos, or men in little boats. Avoid using words like "titillation." Do not add special emphasis to words like "hard."

If you're taking her to play miniature golf, don't make cracks about the blue balls you're using on the course.

Yes, we all miss *Beavis and Butt-Head*, the early 1990s MTV creation in which two stupid teens giggled inanely at words that have double (sexual) meanings. You know who *doesn't* miss those guys right now? The young lady who has agreed, against her better judgment, to go out on a date with you.

Her friends told her that you're a guy with eight hands and two brain cells, and now you're proving it. Would you like to know what it's like to make love to an actual woman? Then, stop with the double entendres. Oh, sorry. That means, "Stop making comments that turn ordinary words into dirty words."

UNWRITTEN RULE #92: A gentleman should avoid sexual innuendo when first dating a woman.

PIGS DO NOT RULE

It's the twenty-first century, yet you are like one of those soldiers on a south seas island who has no idea the war ended decades ago. Well, the war *has* ended, and the male chauvinist pigs lost. They held sway for centuries, convincing women that they were second-class citizens and mental midgets. All the while, Y-chromosome-bearing beings gathered the spoils of living in a man's, man's, man's, man's world.

Well, get off your island, you uncouth d-bag. If you're on a date, open doors for her. Ask her about her job. If you've been dating for a while, then remember that she gets tired, too, after a hard day of work.

Her way of unwinding may be sitting on the couch with you, watching a chick flick. Just deal with it. The movie may suck, but you will get tremendous amounts of credit (read: kinky new bedroom stuff) for being attentive to her needs on a regular basis.

UNWRITTEN RULE #93: A gentleman should never be a male chauvinist pig.

SHE'S NOT YOUR MOM

All women become like their mothers. That is their tragedy. No man does. That's his.
—OSCAR WILDE

You can take care of yourself, and if you can't, then you've got some serious problems (beyond your looks, your personality, your crappy job, etc.). Some men seem to think that relationships are nothing more than an opportunity to gain a new mom who also grants sexual favors. (God, you're a sick bastard.)

Your girlfriend/wife/significant other works hard, too. She has to take care of herself and (possibly) your children. She doesn't need to have another "special delivery" in the home, one who's old enough to shave, drive, and wake up on Sunday mornings with his head in the toilet bowl.

There's nothing wrong with a relationship being a partnership. In fact, that's the way a relationship should work. However, the partnership has to be 50-50 (in case you're not sure, that means each of you has the same amount of responsibility). You can take, but you also must give. Otherwise, she'll leave you for a grown-up.

UNWRITTEN RULE #94: A gentleman should never treat his girlfriend/wife/significant other like she is his mother.

BE HANDY AROUND THE HOUSE, NOT ON A FIRST DATE

Give a man a free hand, and he'll run it all over you.
—MAE WEST

No woman with an IQ over 60 really believes that you're "accidentally" brushing her boobs with your elbow, hand, other (nonintimate) body part. That whole "arm around shoulder in order to squeeze a breast" trick was old when the Pilgrims landed at Plymouth Rock.

Even though mores have changed significantly in the past several decades, you're still better off holding those hormones in check on the first date. Women understand that men are wolves sporting a thin veneer of gentlemanliness. They know what you're hoping for, but they don't want you to act like that's all you want.

Here's an idea: Let her touch you first. Pay attention to her, and pick up on signals. Don't worry. Women are pretty clear because they understand that most men are pretty slow and stupid, really. You'll get what you want eventually, but, in the meantime, you might learn that you actually like the young lady you're with as more than just a chance for some strange. Or, as hard to believe as this may be, you may decide that she's bad news, and you'll choose to avoid any future contact whatsoever.

UNWRITTEN RULE #95: A gentleman should keep his hormones in check on a first date.

DON'T TALK ABOUT WHAT'S-HER-NAME

It's your first date, and all you can talk about is your ex-girlfriend, the one who tore out your heart, sliced it with a razor, poured rubbing alcohol and lemon juice on it, stomped it into squishy muck, and left it in the gutter amid lipstick-stained cigarette butts?

You're supposed to forget about her. That's why you're dating again, remember? That woman with you? She wouldn't have agreed to go out with you if she hadn't found you at least moderately attractive.

She doesn't want to know about that evil witch! She wants you to focus on *her*. If you can't have a conversation without bringing up your disloyal, gorge-inducing ex, then you should go back home, lick your wounds, and wait a while before you get back out there.

UNWRITTEN RULE #96: A gentleman should avoid speaking about his ex-girlfriend on first dates with a new lady.

BE SERIOUS!

Husbands are like fires: They go out when unattended.
—ZSA ZSA GABOR

Women like guys with a sense of humor. In fact, that's one reason she hangs around with you. It's certainly not for your lack of grooming, your dead-end job, or your mother fixation. Nonetheless, some guys just don't know when to turn off the smart-ass tap. Women do *not* like this.

Let's say she comes home after a hard day at work. She's talking about how her boss made her look bad in front of everyone else. That is not the time to put a sock on your hand, pretend it's a puppet, and make rude/obscene remarks.

You need to fine-tune until you attain the perfect balance of ribaldry and sincerity. Even though you may not be as sensitive as she is, you know when she's not in the mood for humor. At those times, try a little sympathy: "Oh, I'll bet that made you feel really angry when he tore apart your presentation in front of everyone, and you worked so hard on it!"

Don't worry. You can still make obscene hand puppets. Just measure her mood first.

UNWRITTEN RULE #97: A gentleman should be serious and sincere when that is the response a lady needs.

ACCEPT YOUR LIMITATIONS

Just because you're fixated on the DIY Network doesn't mean you actually have stopped being all thumbs. Sure, those folks make it look easy to add a sunroom to your home or build a palatial treehouse on a 300-year-old oak. First off, they're experts. Secondly, they didn't *actually* build that sunroom in thirty minutes, and finally, if any big mistakes are made, they can be edited out.

In real life, there are no re-takes. If you destroy the kitchen, *This New House*'s Amy Matthews isn't going to show up and save your sorry ass. You're on the hook for all the repair costs and for all the (much-deserved) grief you will get from your girlfriend/wife/significant other.

It's okay to be completely useless around the house. You've got other, positive qualities (at least we hope you do). You're great, say, at giving backrubs or cooking burgers on the grill or at making just the right joke at just the right time. Accept your limitations, and don't destroy your house (or relationship).

UNWRITTEN RULE #98: A gentleman should always accept his limitations.

THEY'RE CALLED "DIRECTIONS"

I doubt whether any girl would be satisfied with her lover's mind if she knew the whole of it.
—ANTHONY TROLLOPE

We don't care that it's a cliché. We feel it necessary to address the age-old problem that results from primitive man's hunting-and-gathering tendencies. Ever since we rose out of the primordial ooze (for those of us who have, that is), we men have wanted to *find* stuff. We sure as heck don't want to ask where to find stuff.

After all, did Og have to go to the store to get directions to his cave-mother-in-law's house? Hell, no! Og surveyed the prairies, followed faint traces of footpaths, and finally wound up where he needed to be. Today's man is even more sophisticated (by and large) than Og. He doesn't need GPS systems, maps, or any of the rest of that namby-pamby stuff. He has a built-in GPS system, by God!

Okay, okay … Now, let's get back to reality. No, dude. You *don't* have some magical sense of direction. Just because you know that Texas is west of your present location doesn't mean you know exactly how to get to the Alamo.

When you insist on not asking for directions, you look silly, get yelled at, and possibly put everyone's life in danger by winding up on the proverbial wrong side of the tracks. Stop being a caveman. Stop and ask for help.

UNWRITTEN RULE #99: A gentleman should always be willing to accept that he's lost and to ask for directions.

THEY'RE CALLED "DIRECTIONS," PART TWO

Don't be fooled. "Easy assembly required" means that you need only a master's in engineering to put together your son's Christmas present. "Some assembly required" indicates a PhD is a prerequisite for getting the thing put together in fewer than twenty-four hours.

Whatever you do, don't be a typical guy and blithely toss aside the assembly instructions. They are *not* optional. When Jimmy wakes up to find his bicycle under the tree, you'll be a hero. If, instead, Jimmy wakes up to find "Santa" sitting on the floor near the tree, surrounded by various bicycle parts and a few empty cans of beer, you will destroy not only his belief in holiday magic but his belief in you as well. Merry Christmas, stupid.

UNWRITTEN RULE #100: A gentleman should always follow directions when assembling something.

YOUR FRIENDS DON'T NEED TO KNOW EVERYTHING

Locker room talk is *so* middle school. Then, you were bullshitting your friends into believing you were getting action. Now that you're in a relationship and actually are getting some, you still want to tell your friends all about it. Dude, that's just crass.

Think about it. Do you want her to tell *her* friends about your "shortcomings" or about your fumbling and inept attempts at foreplay or about your inability to make the act last longer than eight seconds? Yeah, we thought not.

One thing that makes a couple a couple is intimacy, and we're not just talking about sex. You two should not have secrets from each other, but you should have secrets from your friends. Yes, it may cause some distance to grow between you and your pals, but that's just because they're jealous d-bags.

Man up, and keep your mouth shut.

UNWRITTEN RULE #101: A gentleman should never engage in "locker room talk" about his paramour.

INTIMACY DOES NOT EQUAL SEX

When women talk about "connecting" with their mate, we men get confused. The wheezy squirrel or injured ferret or whatever rodent it is that turns the wheel in our brain comes up with only one conclusion: "Oh, she wants to have sex."

When we start to move toward you, making overtures, you turn away in disgust. We feel hurt. Possibly, we say/do something stupid. Well, we're always doing that. We say/do something egregiously stupid.

Men, here's the deal. *Intimacy* means "closeness." Sure, sex may evolve from closeness, but it doesn't have to. You have a specific end in mind. A young lady does not. She just wants to be held and petted. She wants to feel like you're there for her, that she's the most important person/place/thing in your life. Often, that just means hold her and shut up.

UNWRITTEN RULE #102: A gentleman should understand that intimacy and sex are not the same thing.

THUGS ARE STUPID

I want a man who's kind and understanding. Is that too much to ask of a millionaire?

—ZSA ZSA GABOR

The, um, fashion that began in the late 1990s—pants halfway down one's ass with big ol' bloomers showing—should have disappeared before it had a chance to sprout, like a pestilence or too much Axe Body Spray, from the bodies of sullen teens across the country.

Yeah, yeah. You're a thug. It doesn't matter that you live in the suburbs or spent fifty bucks on "just the right" boxers to display above your $100 pair of jeans. It doesn't matter that, in middle age, photos of you in all your "glory" could be used as blackmail by your parents, who smirk at the knowledge that even *you* now realize how preposterous you looked.

The sagging trend doesn't just end with an insult to the world of sartorial splendor, though. Most teens and young men who adopt this look also feel the need to act like "tough guys" (read: chauvinistic, navel-gazing a-holes). So, your butt crack is on display *and* you're acting like a butt-head. Nice, real nice. Grow the "f" up already.

UNWRITTEN RULE #103: A gentleman should eschew the "thug" look and thuggish behavior.

85

PUT ON A SHIRT, PLEASE

You've got pecs of steel (a head to match) and washboard abs. How do we know? Because you never seem to wear a freaking shirt, dude. When we see you jogging down the street? No shirt. When we see you working in your yard? No shirt. Jeez, no shirt even when we come by to borrow your leafblower. Yeah, yeah, you look great, but you make us feel fat and jealous and . . . to tell you the truth, just a little bit awkward. Should we notice that you look great?

Perhaps if we actually looked good naked, we would be fine with you going around half-naked all the time. But, the thing is, we don't look good naked. Most Americans don't. That's why we hate you *and* your toned guts.

Try wearing a shirt that's two sizes too small or something. Then, you still get to show off your hard-earned body, and we don't have to feel jealous (or slightly gay) around you. And, whatever you do, stay the hell away from our wife/girlfriend/significant other if you're going to insist on being topless.

UNWRITTEN RULE #104: A gentleman should always wear a shirt.

UNFLAGGING FLATULENCE

Women fart. Surely they do. Nonetheless, they seem to have better control over their digestive systems and their sphincters. Guys, on the other hand, have a tendency to fart and belch constantly. How can one (slightly to severely out-of-shape) body contain so much gas? Dang, we're the answer to the world's energy crisis.

While we concur with ancient wisdom (we think Confucius or Lao Tzu or perhaps assorted members of the Irish race said this)—that it's better to let it out and bear the shame than keep it in and bear the pain—we also must urge you to strike a blow in favor of common decency.

If you can't keep those ass bombs to yourself, then at least step away from the decent, God-fearing, olfactory-possessing folks in your immediate vicinity. Let fly and then return to society. And while it may be a cool parlor trick, we urge you not to belch the alphabet in mixed company, such as, say, when you're first meeting your girlfriend's parents.

UNWRITTEN RULE #105: A gentleman should be courteous in relation to belching and flatulence.

OPEN THE DOOR

A man snatches the first kiss, pleads for the second, demands the third, takes the fourth, accepts the fifth—and endures all the rest.
—HELEN ROWLAND, JOURNALIST AND HUMORIST

We witness regularly the witless actions of stupid men. They accompany a woman (an actual woman, willing to go out with them) to the door of a club/restaurant/movie theater and then walk on through. Often, they don't even hold the door for their companions, let alone open the door for them to go through first.

Wow, even cavemen, best known for knocking prospective mates on the head and dragging them by the hair to their lairs, would have followed the "open doors for the ladies" rule if doors had existed. There's probably cave art that depicts this custom. Opening the damn door isn't an unwritten rule so much as it's simple common sense, which may be the problem now that we think about it. You can't use what you don't have.

Open doors. We don't care that we exist in a new "enlightened" world and all that. Most women, if honest, would admit that they *like* having doors—car doors, restaurant doors, door doors—opened for them. And if appealing to common sense doesn't work, keep in mind that demonstrating a soupcon of common courtesy may actually get you into her bedroom sooner rather than never.

UNWRITTEN RULE #106: A gentleman should always open doors for his female companions.

LET HER LEAD THE WAY

Nowadays, most guys don't even bother to open doors for their dates or female companions (see above). Perhaps they believe that modern women consider this act outdated and sexist, rather than chivalric. More likely, they're just selfish banana slugs.

Although many of the great Emily Post's entreaties to men regarding the "fairer sex" *are* outdated and sexist, some of them still deserve to be recognized. Among them is the act of letting a young lady lead the way.

Picture this: You escort a woman (your sister, your date, a call girl, doesn't matter) into a restaurant by opening the door for her. Once both of you are inside the establishment, you should not jockey for position. Don't race around her to the hostess stand. Don't push her out of the way to get to the counter at Waffle House. Don't walk fifteen steps ahead of her as though she actually belongs with another party.

Let her lead the way. Show deference to her needs. Jeez, just act like you've got a lick of sense and a dollop of courtesy somewhere within your immature heart.

UNWRITTEN RULE #107: A gentleman should always follow his female companion into buildings and let her lead the way.

TEMPER IN CHECK

Men have been emasculated in our culture to some extent. They wear suits and ties, rather than carry clubs or spears. They can get manicures and wear earrings without most people questioning their sexual orientation. They don't play sports; they play videogames that feature sports.

Perhaps that's why some men spoil for a chance to fight. Their DNA has not helped them to evolve much past caveman status (or, in some cases, past Neanderthal status). Consequently, they like to lose their temper, often in inappropriate situations.

For example, if someone is threatening your wife and kids, then, yes, go medieval on them. If, on the other hand, someone cuts you off in traffic, you are *not* in the right to tailgate that person while honking your horn, raising your middle finger, and screaming at the top of your lungs.

When you lose your temper, you do not come across as strong. You come across as a scared little psychotic bully. A man who can remain in control of himself at all times gives off an aura of strength, even if he's actually quite the opposite.

The bottom line, you see, is that it's all about appearances. Manicures have practically become unisex, but a guy losing his shit for no really good reason remains both masculine and sad, very, very sad . . . pathetic, in fact.

UNWRITTEN RULE #108: A gentleman should keep his temper in check at all times.

AVERT THOSE BEADY EYES

A gentleman is simply a patient wolf.
—LANA TURNER, ACTRESS

If you manage to avoid a "hot war," don't get involved in a "cold war" either. Allowing things to heat up into yelling and throwing punches is trailer trash stuff, the sort of thing you see on reality TV shows that deal with "the men and women of law enforcement."

A cold war takes place with the eyes. Some guy does something you find reprehensible, so you stare at him, focusing your beady eyes on him, attempting desperately to turn your gaze into a laser beam so that you can blow that a-hole's head clean off.

Mature men will walk away from a staring contest, realizing they stop being cool by about age seven. They understand that these visual pissing matches accomplish nothing. Some, however, may take the bait, and in no time, a simple misunderstanding or inadvertent jerk-off move on someone's part can escalate into a public brawl.

If someone does something stupid, just ignore it. If someone does something egregiously stupid, then simply point out the problem in a neutral tone and move on. Staring daggers at someone is the wrong way to go.

UNWRITTEN RULE #109: A gentleman should never hold another gentleman with an angry stare over a real or perceived slight.

HATS OFF!

Gentlemen no longer wear top hats, but they love their fitted baseball caps, usually worn with the price tag still attached to demonstrate the hat is, in fact, new. Sometimes they're worn correctly, but most of the time, these caps are worn to the side or even backward. Let's not mince words: They look freaking ridiculous.

Nonetheless, though headgear of today has lost its elegance, it is certainly omnipresent. Men have forgotten that hats should not be worn inside, especially in the presence of ladies. Sure, we understand that many men wear these caps to hide thinning hair and bald spots, but are they *really* expecting to get more booty for wearing caps that advertise an obsession with losing sports teams?

Doff your cap while indoors. It shows respect and a scrap of taste. If you lack these things, then taking off your hat indoors can fool people (i.e., women) into thinking you have some taste and respect.

UNWRITTEN RULE #110: A gentleman always removes his hat indoors and in the presence of a lady.

GIVE IT UP

SCENE: A crowded bus. No seats are available.

Men sit sprawled alone in seats designed for at least two people. They have earbuds stuck firmly into their vacuous heads. As far as they're concerned, no one exists on the planet except for them.

A woman, JENNY, carrying a baby, enters the bus at one stop. She has been working all day and has just retrieved her little boy from daycare. She's exhausted. After looking up to determine that she's not worth flirting with (dude, she's already got a kid, yo), they go back to their mindlessness.

Finally, from the back, JOHNNY speaks.

JOHNNY: Ma'am, would you like to have my seat?

JENNY: Oh, that's okay.

JOHNNY: No, I insist. Here, let me help you.

JOHNNY gives up his seat to JENNY, like a good gentleman. Two years later, he is struck and killed by a wayward meteor and goes straight to heaven, a place reserved for all gentlemen who understand courtesy and civility.

**UNWRITTEN RULE #111: When no seats
are available, a gentleman always gives up
his seat to a lady or to his elders.**

DO YOU NEED ANYTHING?

Women are never disarmed by compliments; men always are.
—OSCAR WILDE

Most women, if they answered honestly, would say that four little words are more important to them than three little words. "I love you" can become a manipulative declaration. Some men use these words as foreplay, for example, or the words can be said in place of an apology after a man has done something egregiously stupid.

But the words "do you need anything?" demonstrate that a man is thinking of his wife's/girlfriend's/significant other's needs. They indicate concern and caring, and they give you major brownie points, which can be turned in the next time you do something egregiously stupid.

For example, let's say you're going into the kitchen for a beer. Ask your special lady, "Do you need anything?" She might reply, "No." You still get the points. Or, she might say, "Yes, I'd like a white wine, please." Get your beer, pour her a wine, and you have quickly and easily increased your get-some-this-evening potential exponentially.

We're not saying you shouldn't say, "I love you." Some guys have trouble getting out these words, and they *do* mean a lot to your significant other. We're just suggesting that you add the question, "Do you need anything?" to your repertoire.

UNWRITTEN RULE #112: A gentleman should make frequent use of the question, "Do you need anything?" when interacting with his wife/girlfriend/significant other.

A-ROUND AND ROUND IT GOES

Nobody likes a lizard-brained sap, and anyone who refuses to pay for a round of drinks is the aforementioned reptilian drain. Some days, however, you may legitimately not have the funds necessary to buy a round. It happens. Other guys can understand this. What other guys cannot abide is when you withhold this information until it's your turn to pay up.

We suggest that you and your buddies devise a round-buying system *before* you head off to your local tavern to drink too much, bitch about work/women/the inadequate performance of your local sports team(s), and make fools of yourselves at the karaoke machine.

Decide, in advance, whose turn it is to start buying rounds. If no agreement can be reached—and guys are very good at coming up with reasons why it shouldn't be their turn this time, even when it patently *should* be—then agree on some method for choosing: rock/paper/scissors, arm wrestling, whatever.

Next, agree on the round-buying order. You might also consider deciding, in advance, how many rounds you will buy. Agree that, if anyone wants to go beyond that number, he will have to shell out for his own swill.

Finally, make sure you tell the group in advance that you are short of cash and cannot contribute to the evening's brew this week. Agree—hell, make a blood oath if necessary—that you'll buy two rounds next time, and then actually buy the two rounds the next time.

UNWRITTEN RULE #113: Gentlemen should have discussions in advance regarding the buying of rounds in a drinking establishment.

CHAPTER 4

UNWRITTEN RULES

FOR WOMEN

Ah, women. We love you. You just naturally seem to possess breeding that men lack. You tend to have wonderful grooming and personal hygiene. You always remember to send thank-you cards and holiday cards and get-well cards. Let's face it: When a card is required, you're Joanie on the spot.

BUT.

You're also, in your own fashion, just as—if not more—selfish than men. You're prone to jealousy. Granted, you're often right to have your doubts, but sometimes he's actually being good when he's out of your sight. You also can be clingy, bitchy, supercilious, holier-than-thou, and a whole host of other qualities of which Emily Post would not approve.

Please pay attention to the following unwritten rules, which will all-but guarantee better interpersonal relationships with friends and lovers. Follow them, and you will find the men in your life more attentive and less likely to shut down in your presence. Ignore them, and you will be that woman in your apartment building who hoards bobby pins and cats, lots and lots of cats.

CALL WHEN YOU'VE ACTUALLY GOT SOMETHING TO SAY

We love hearing from you . . . when you've got something to say. Men talk to communicate, not to share feelings or "feel connected" (whatever that means exactly). If we get a call, we expect to receive or impart information.

The truth is, ladies, when you call a man "just to talk," he gets annoyed because he thinks you're checking up on him, making sure he isn't up to no good, or even hoping to catch him with his hand in the proverbial honey pot.

A gentleman might also get annoyed because "I just want to talk" generally includes the unspoken words "about what a jerk I think you've been." And most guys don't really want to ruminate over—much less talk about—what a jerk you think they've been.

UNWRITTEN RULE #114: A lady should only call a gentleman when she has something substantive to say.

MY MOOD HAS NOTHING TO DO WITH YOU

A lousy day at work. Some ★@%!% who cut you off in traffic. Learning that an old friend just got a prestigious award while you're still stuck in cubicle hell watching your life run out with every tap of a keyboard.

Any of these scenarios can put a gentleman into a funk. In fact, days come along when *all* of the above happen in horrifying succession, like some hellish set of bone-carved dominoes.

The point is, when all of these things happen, a gentleman will be in a bad mood, and—for better or worse—most men prefer to simmer in silence rather than to talk about how these things made them feel.

Just give him a moment, ladies. Let him wind down. Eventually, he'll start to vent to you. Just give him some space and—whatever you do—don't make the mistake of thinking that he's upset about you. If you assume something like that, you'll get upset, and his mood—which has nothing to do with you—will escalate into an argument involving you both.

UNWRITTEN RULE #115: A lady should never assume that a gentleman's foul mood has anything at all to do with her.

YOU ARE NOT FINE

Here's to women. Would that we could fall into her arms without falling into her hands.
—AMBROSE BIERCE, AUTHOR

"Are you okay? What's wrong?"

"Nothing. I'm fine."

Screech.

No, you're not. Men aren't completely clueless and devoid of feelings. We understand nuance and tone better than you think. We know you're *not* really "fine."

The problem is that we don't know why you're not fine. Probably, we think, it's got something to do with us. We must have said or done (or you assume, probably correctly, that we said or did) something stupid and thoughtless. We get that part. We just don't know what we did.

Please, don't keep us in the dark. Explain the error of our ways, in as nonjudgmental a manner as possible, and, most likely, we will respond positively.

UNWRITTEN RULE #116: A lady should never say she is "fine" when she is upset. She should explain the issue in a nonjudgmental manner.

ISN'T SAYING IT 100 TIMES ENOUGH?

Men wander around pretty much safe in the knowledge that their girlfriend/wife/significant other loves them if they've said so at some point. Unless we're told otherwise, we don't see any reason why anything should change regarding your affection.

That's why men don't understand when women seem to need constant reminding that their boyfriend/husband/significant other still loves them. "Of course," we think. "We told you we did last week." Or, "Of course. Didn't you notice how I did a pretty good job of cleaning up after I yakked in the sink? If I didn't love you, I would have let *you* clean up all those chunks."

Ladies, please take a page from your men. Unless you have a genuine reason to doubt, then you can just assume that your lover still loves you.

UNWRITTEN RULE #117: A lady should not constantly ask her lover if he still loves her.

PMS DOES NOT REQUIRE EDGINESS

Even though men do not understand menstruation and many of them are terrified of it, they do understand the concept of PMS: premenstrual syndrome. We know that if (The horror! The horror!) you ask us to pick up some pads on our way home from work, that we can expect you to be a tad edgy.

Nonetheless, some of us have become pretty sure that PMS is just an excuse to act . . . well, let's just say, *extremely* edgy and foul-tempered. Raging fights can erupt over innocent questions like, "What's for dinner?" or "Can I have the remote?"

No, we don't know what menstrual cramps feel like, and we're pretty sure we don't want to, either. Nonetheless, give us a little break, please? We want to help you feel better but not if you're going to use PMS like a bludgeon.

UNWRITTEN RULE #118: A lady should not use PMS as an excuse to act foul-tempered and pick fights.

WHY ELSE WOULD YOU BE DRESSED LIKE THAT?

We have drugs to make women speak but none to keep them silent.

—ANATOLE FRANCE, AUTHOR

Booty shorts. Navel-peek T's. Hemlines that show legs up to there. These send one message to guys: We are ready for sex. When we are confronted with another message—Keep your filthy hands off me, and how dare you assume that you're going to get some!—then we are confused and, quite possibly, upset.

We're not saying you can't dress however you choose. All we're saying is please don't get upset with us if we make certain assumptions when you're dressed provocatively. We can't help it. We're men. When we're not thinking about work or sports, we're thinking about sex. When you look sexy, we forget all about work and sports.

UNWRITTEN RULE #119: A lady should not be upset if, when dressed provocatively, her boyfriend/husband/ significant other assumes she is in the mood for sex.

DRAMA IS A CLASS IN HIGH SCHOOL

Someone disrespected you? What does that even mean?!? Life is too short to take offense at possible slights.

Sure, a man may get upset if someone does something like try to steal his girl or his beer, but, basically, we're live and let live. If someone confronts us, we settle the score through debate and discussion (at least that's what a gentleman *should* do).

We don't feel the need to share our business on a social networking website. We don't spend hours on the phone with our friends parsing out each moment of a third-hand conversation. Life is too short. Leave drama to Romeo and Juliet, please.

UNWRITTEN RULE #120: A lady should never engage in "drama."

THIS IS NOT THE TIME

Ah, the post-coital glow. We had one. We're pretty sure you had one, but we could be wrong. We should care, but . . . Anyway, that's not the point. Here's the problem.

As we lie there peacefully, you start to bring up finances or an argument we had three days ago (that we thought was dealt with already). Suddenly, our mellow is harshed. In fact, we feel somewhat manipulated.

Men are completely bamboozled by women's ability to bring up challenging conversational gambits at what we feel are *exactly* the wrong time. For us, post-coital time is for relaxation and connection, not discord.

UNWRITTEN RULE #121: A lady should never bring up challenging topics right after sex.

SHUT OFF THE WATERWORKS

If women didn't exist, all the money in the
world would have no meaning.
—ARISTOTLE ONASSIS

We're not saying that men never cry. If a man's team loses a big game in the final moments due to a bad call, then, sure, he will cry, after he's through screaming obscenities. But men rarely use tears to get their way.

Some women, however, have made a religion of this process.

You're arguing about something that doesn't seem very important when, wham, she begins to cry and reproach you for things you aren't sure are 100 percent legitimate. But what difference does that make? She's crying, and *you* caused it to happen. Chances are, you'll give in to whatever she demands.

Ladies, this is not fair. It's called manipulation. Even though tears usually work, they ultimately drive a wedge between you and your man.

UNWRITTEN RULE #122: A lady should never use crocodile tears as a form of manipulation.

OTHER PEOPLE EXIST

It's true! They really, really do! Your needs are not the only needs on planet Earth!

Everyone is selfish from time to time. It's just human nature. However, if you're one of those women who cannot see past the end of her nose, then you are doing a disservice to humanity. You're perpetuating the stereotype that women are completely selfish and self-centered.

Even other women, who are *not* selfish and self-centered, probably hate you for skewering perceptions. Just remember that there are many sides to any given situation, and while yours is certainly important, it's not the only one that matters.

UNWRITTEN RULE #123: A lady should never be selfish and self-centered.

MAXING OUT

Retail therapy is not necessarily a bad thing, just as tossing a few dollars in a slot machine does not make someone a gambler. If, however, someone uses next month's mortgage because he's just sure that a huge jackpot is imminent, then he's not just a gambler, he's a thoughtless, selfish a-hole whose compulsion has a negative impact on the rest of his family.

Yes, we're trying to draw a parallel between that guy and you, the woman who maxes out a Whitman's Sampler of plastic in an effort to cheer herself up after one of life's routine disappointments. Buying a pair of shoes because you're depressed is fine. Buying a shoe store because you're depressed is not.

UNWRITTEN RULE #124: A lady should never max out her credit cards while engaging in retail therapy.

MEN ARE NOT SMART ENOUGH TO READ MINDS

Women are more difficult than men. It's their minds.

—PETER SELLERS

Ladies, we know you don't think we're capable of putting down toilet seats, peeing with doors closed, or drinking beverages out of tumblers. So, why do you think we can read minds?!?

If a gentleman asks, "What's wrong?" then he's seeking information. He really doesn't know what's wrong, only that he, most likely, had something to do with the situation that has made you all lachrymose.

Responding, "You should know," is not helpful. Perhaps we *should* know, but we don't. We're not really all that bright, and we certainly can't read your mind or anybody else's. We want to make things right, but we can't even start to do that if you expect us to figure out, on our own, how we screwed up this time.

UNWRITTEN RULE #125: A lady should always remember that gentlemen cannot read minds.

NAGS ARE FOR THE RACE TRACK

Yes, men *do* have a tendency to procrastinate, and they are masters at the game of "not me."

"Hey, whose turn it is to buy a round?"

"Not me, I got it last time."

"Not me, I bought the burgers."

"Not me, I'm broke."

Be that as it may, men do not respond to repeated requests for action, also known as "nagging."

We understand that you asked us three weeks ago to fix the screened-in porch or to send your mom a thank-you card or to take you out to that fancy new restaurant. We honestly *do* intend to grant your request, and, yes, we should be more solicitous of your requests in the first place. But nagging won't make your wishes come true any faster. It will just irk us to the point of petulance, and we will refuse to grant your requests at all.

Here's a possible solution: Write down your needs on a list, and put that list in a conspicuous place, such as on the refrigerator or on top of our porn stash. We will appreciate not only that you have needs but also that you are expressing them without nagging us.

UNWRITTEN RULE #126: A lady should never nag a gentleman.

WHATEVER YOU WANT

Young men, in the grip of first love, may make the rookie mistake of lending credence to the words "whatever you want." Woe be to them if they do!

These words actually are intended to point out that your lady love believes you are being selfish. Allow us to translate the phrase: "Let's just do whatever you want because that's all we ever do. You don't really care about *my* needs or feelings. You're a selfish jerk, and I'm not sure why I'm with you in the first place."

Ladies, we understand that some men—many men—are, in fact, selfish jerks. Nonetheless, men only understand direct communication. Sorry, we're just kind of slow that way. We constantly marvel at your ability to communicate telepathically with your female friends. Unfortunately, our "Y" chromosome appears to block that ability.

Just tell us what you want. Stand up for yourself. Give us a reason why you have your needs. Be very straightforward. Treat us like we're ten years old.

UNWRITTEN RULE #127: A lady should never use the phrase "whatever you want," when she does not really mean it.

YOU CAN'T FIX HIM

Women should not be enlightened or educated in any way.
They should, in fact, be segregated as they are the cause
of hideous and involuntary erections in holy men.
—ST. AUGUSTINE

Many women are in the grip of a fantasy. They honestly believe that, through their beneficent power, they can transform horse manure into a knight on a shining steed.

He's not bad; he's misunderstood. He's just waiting for the right woman. He *needs* me. He'll change; just wait and see.

If you are a woman who has ever thought or made one of the previous statements, then we have news for you: You are delusional. Bad boys never change. If he sleeps around now, he will sleep around even after he has met your wonderful self. If he acted like his last girlfriend didn't exist, then he'll treat you the same way.

We're sorry you've been brainwashed by chick flicks. We're just trying to give you a bracing dose of truth, girlfriend.

UNWRITTEN RULE #128: A lady should never get with a "bad boy" in anticipation of transforming him into a nice guy.

WHEN DID WE GET ON THAT SUBJECT?

Men tend to compartmentalize their feelings and experiences. One incident is kept here. Another incident is stored there. These two incidents, though sharing some similarities perhaps, have no connection to one another, as far as your average man is concerned. Our minds are like computers from the 1950s: slow and not very sophisticated.

Women's minds, on the other hand, are amazing. Every piece of information, every feeling, every experience is intertwined and intricately connected. It's nothing short of amazing. Miraculous, actually.

The problems arise during arguments. Men become bamboozled, baffled, and bewildered when a discussion about not taking out the trash becomes a diatribe about something that happened four years ago that had nothing whatsoever to do with trash. And then *that* morphs into a reminder of our shortcomings in bed (not enough foreplay, not enough post-coital cuddling).

Men get angry at some point because we are so confused. We have no clue how we got from trash to foreplay. When confused, men tend to lash out in anger. Please, ladies. Just give us a roadmap, okay?

Pretend that we are not very bright, even if we possess a PhD in astrophysics. Connect the dots for us. The results will be better understanding between partners.

UNWRITTEN RULE #129: A lady should always help a gentleman understand how she gets from subject A to subject E without passing through subjects B, C, and D.

WHY DO YOU LOOK/SMELL LIKE A HO?

Makeup is designed to bring out a woman's natural beauty, but nature has never produced shocking blue, chartreuse, puce, or ecru eyelids. It may produce red lips, but it eschews neon scarlet lips, and only raccoons seem to sport a superfluity of mascara (and is raccoon *really* the look you're going for?).

Likewise, perfume is designed to be subtle . . . unless it's cheap. Then it's formulated to have all the subtlety of a four-man rush defense. A little dab will do you, and even then it's overpowering. If you shower in it, then you'll knock down everyone in the room.

We're not here to judge "ladies of the pavement." They do their jobs to make money for their needs like everyone else. But, if you're not a prostitute, then why do you choose to look and/or smell like one? Ease up on the face paint. Spend money on real perfume, and, once you buy it, don't bathe in it.

UNWRITTEN RULE #130: A lady should use a modest amount of makeup and perfume.

DON'T BE DUMB (UNLESS YOU ARE)

Brigands demand your money or your life; women require both.
—SAMUEL BUTLER

Men are dumb (i.e., can't dress or groom themselves, helpless on their own, one-track minds), even the smart ones (e.g., atomic bombs, global warming, cheez in a can). The law of averages indicates that some women *must* be dumb as well, but far more act dumb, and this puzzles us.

Are these women afraid that dumb men only find dumb women attractive? If so, then that makes sense. But some women just seem to act dumb for no really good reason. They giggle at stupid remarks. They act like they've never read Jane Austen (or even a stop sign). They put the capital letters in "DITZ."

Ladies, please stop. If you truly lack enough brain power to open a Happy Meal, that's fine. If, however, you are brilliant *and* beautiful, just be brilliant. Smart men may be capable of dumb ideas (e.g., jihad, smart bombs, SPAM), but they still like to be with smart women. Maybe, with your help, you can stop SPAM and cheez in a can.

UNWRITTEN RULE #131: A smart lady should never act dumb in order to attract a man.

FISH IN THE POND, NOT FOR COMPLIMENTS

This may not be the number one rule, as far as guys are concerned, but it's certainly in the top five: Men don't like to be manipulated. Sure, we're easy to manipulate, and as long as you're subtle about it, you're fine.

If, however, you make your manipulation obvious, then even *men* will figure out what's going on after a while. One case in point is the fishing pond of compliments. You've gotten a new dress, and it's smokin' hot. We probably notice it, think to say something about it, then get sidetracked by another thought (Grunt. Me hungry. Grunt.).

Since we've failed to notice your new dress, you start to make comments suggesting you "look different" or something. After a while, we get it. We forgot to make the comment about your appearance, but since we did and since you're now fishing for a compliment, we men will get stupid and childish and refuse to say anything.

If you could just give us a little bit of time, we promise we'll notice you and make the appropriate comment. If we don't by the time we take you home, then you can let us have it (a lecture, not, you know, "it").

UNWRITTEN RULE #132: A lady should never fish for compliments from a gentleman.

HE HASN'T CHANGED

*A man must be potent and orgasmic to ensure the future
of the race. A woman only needs to be available.*
—MASTERS AND JOHNSON, SEX RESEARCHERS

Most creatures evolve, but evolution is a glacially slow process. Unfortunately, some creatures—like your ex-boyfriend—never evolve. When you met him, he was a poorly groomed, consistently inconsistent, womanizing, chauvinist pig. Then, he met you. After several months/years, he remained a poorly groomed, consistently inconsistent, womanizing, chauvinist pig.

You parted ways. Since then, for some reason, you find yourself missing him. You imagine that his time with you *must* have had a positive impact; you just didn't give the seeds you planted time to grow. You track him down (not too difficult ... still living in the basement of his mother's house), and declare an interest in reconnecting. He belches, rubs himself, and says, "Yeah, whatever."

Now, weeks later, you learn that he's still a poorly groomed, consistently inconsistent, etc. Ladies, men don't change. Until Jesus or Buddha or Vishnu swoops out of the sky and taps your guy on the shoulder, he will remain the human equivalent of a one-cell amoeba who will never evolve onto dry land.

**UNWRITTEN RULE #133: A lady should never
go back to an old boyfriend, convinced that
he has changed, because he has not.**

STOP MAKING LIKE NIXON

Richard Nixon wasn't brought down by a bungled robbery. He was brought down by his rampant and unchecked paranoia. Perhaps there's a lesson here for you as well.

For example, if you ask your guy where he's been and he seems evasive, then that doesn't necessarily mean he's been doing anything wrong. Guys have radar for this sort of thing. If he senses you're asking about his whereabouts because you think he was up to no good, then he'll be likely to shut down and become mum.

Granted, he may be evasive because he *has* been up to no good, but unless you've got reason to believe he's skeezing around, give him a pass.

UNWRITTEN RULE #134: A woman should not be paranoid about her guy without good reason.

IT'S JUST SEX

Since the days of chastity belts, men have been led to believe that women are fair, virginal creatures for whom sex is akin to a spiritual act. Slowly, these frigid patches have begun to thaw. If the 1960s proved anything, it's that women like a good roll in the hay as much as any guy.

Yet, to this day, some women who engage in casual sex want to transform the act into something meaningful. They believe that sex is the doorway to a relationship or, in fact, confirms relationship status. Before long, these women begin to assert themselves into men's lives, acting like they have a mystical hold on them.

When bumping uglies leads to assumptions of couplehood, then remind yourself: It was just sex. You knew it at the time, and so did he. Just have fun. Sex happens. Relationships happen. It's all good.

UNWRITTEN RULE #135: A lady should never try to make casual sex into something more than casual sex.

NOTICING DOESN'T MEAN WE'RE CHEATING

Just because we notice the cupcake doesn't mean we're going to lick the icing. Even Shakespeare noted, in *Romeo and Juliet*, "Young men's love then lies / Not truly in their hearts, but in their eyes."

Even when our hearts have been pierced, our eyes aren't blinded. If shawty looked good on the dance floor then, she's going to look good on the dance floor *now*, even though we're holding hands.

Granted, if your guy makes a big deal about noticing other women's attributes, then, sure, you've got cause to smack him upside the head. But if you're in the grocery store and notice him subtly checking out some melons that aren't in the produce aisle, give him a pass.

Forget all that stuff that right wingnuts parrot about lust in your heart being the same thing as cheating. Guys are human. Hell, so are you. Are you really going to say that your eyes never stray when you're at the gym?

UNWRITTEN RULE #136: A lady should remember that a man casually noticing an attractive woman does not necessarily mean that he is cheating.

NOT SO HOLY

Men, we've got news for you. Women, regardless of what they may say or how they may act, actually do sleep around, eat too much, drink too much, and they even leave monstrous bowel movements in the toilet that require multiple flushes.

It's true! It's not just you gentlemen who, on occasion, do these things. Nonetheless, that is what some women would have you believe: that *they* are above reproach while you are, uh, below reproach?

We're not pointing this out to give gentlemen a green light to act like pigs. We're simply pointing out that neither sex should act holier than thou. Ladies, if you can admit that, yes, at times you have lust in your heart or that, on occasion, you like to get trashed and act stupid, then you might give the men in your lives a teensy weensy break when they look at other women (just look, mind you) or tie too many on.

We understand that guilt can make an effective weapon, and if a guy truly deserves to feel guilty, then pile on reproach for all it's worth. If, however, your man just did something you do on occasion, then cut out the high priest routine.

UNWRITTEN RULE #137: A lady should never act "holier than thou" around her gentleman companions.

JEALOUS? NOW?!?

**Women cannot complain about men anymore until
they start getting better taste in them.**

—BILL MAHER

"Hey, my old high school yearbook," Bob says. "I thought I'd lost this thing!"

"Oh, let me see," says Mary.

The couple starts turning yellowing pages. Both laugh at references to long-forgotten nicknames ("Pig Face"), at pictures of long-ago "fashions" (Did women not have real shoulders in the 1980s? Is *that* why they had to wear those shirts with the padded shoulders?), and at pictures of a much-younger—and much less follicly challenged—version of Bob.

The trouble starts when Mary and Bob begin to read through the autograph section.

"What does 'thanks for one of the most memorable nights of my life' mean, Bob?"

"Oh, she was just an old girlfriend. I don't even know if you could say we were a couple. We only dated for, like, three weeks."

Screech.

"Dated? Or screwed like mountain gorillas?"

"Well, yeah, we had sex. I mean, Mary, that was over twenty years ago."

"Do you still love her?"

"I don't know that I ever loved her, really. I . . . "

"Oh, you didn't love her, but she was just dandy for 'memorable nights.'"

Bob, if he's smart, will just shut up now. Mary's off the chain, and she'll run until she gets to the invisible fence. A fun, lighthearted opportunity to share the past has descended quickly into a jealousy fest . . . jealousy over an event from *two decades ago*. Bad. Very bad.

UNWRITTEN RULE #138: A lady should not become jealous (or act jealous) over long-ago incidents in a gentleman's life.

STAY *AWAY* FROM MY STUFF!

Women tend to be communal and sharing; it's one of their greatest qualities. Men, on the other hand, typically are proprietary. In addition, women often consider the sentiments surrounding their possessions; e.g., I love this because you gave it to me on our honeymoon. Men, on the other hand, focus on their possessions as possessions, and they don't want anyone messing with them.

Women and men run into problems when women bring their communal approach to men's stuff. For example, let's say a man and woman decide to move in together. The lady decides to "surprise" her man by replacing the "ugly" lamp he uses with one of her own "pretty" lamps. Most likely, the man will go totally apeshit.

"What happened to my lamp?"

"Well, dear, it was kind of ugly and old, so I replaced it."

"You *what*?!?"

Etc.

Ladies, we're not saying you can't work to bring good taste into your man's life. We're just pointing out that you can't do it through shock and awe. Talk to him about particular items. Lay the ground-work. Don't make a big deal out of it, just let him know how you feel. In time, he'll probably come around and let you fix up the place appropriately.

UNWRITTEN RULE #139: A lady should never treat a gentleman's stuff as *her* stuff without first talking to the gentleman about the item or items.

SEX ISN'T *A* WEAPON

Curve: The loveliest distance between two points.

—MAE WEST

Long before murderous strains of venereal disease existed, women had already figured out that sex makes a great weapon. Men, they realized, would crawl across broken glass and the rotting corpses of cute pup-pies just to "get some."

As a result, women could merely threaten to withhold inter-course, and guys would immediately fall into line: "Yes, dear, of *course* I'd rather spend the weekend with your folks. That hunting trip I've been looking forward to for six months really isn't that important after all."

Human beings may have invented flying machines, "magic" com-munication devices, and Tupperware over the last century or so, but the threat of withheld sex still holds much mojo. Few men can resist its power, and few women can resist wielding its power.

Be that as it may, sex can symbolize all manner of things, but it should never by symbolic of weaponry. "Sex is natural. Sex is fun. Sex is best when it's one on one." Sex is, in short, whatever George Michael says it is, and he *never* said that it's a weapon.

Ladies, tell the men in your life why something matters. Men tend to be stupid. They honestly don't get the nuances of your feelings. They want to do right by you, but they are confused (and, admittedly, often selfish). If you can help them truly understand why something is important to you, then you shouldn't have to use sex as a weapon. The man in your life will, willingly, bow to your wishes. If he doesn't, then he's waste and should be jettisoned like frozen chemical poop from an airplane.

UNWRITTEN RULE #140: A lady should never use sex as a weapon.

CHAPTER 5

UNWRITTEN RULES

FOR EVERYONE

Some unwritten rules pertain primarily to men, others to women, and some to all members of the human race. As a species, we human beings tend to be little island nations. Other animals, when seeing members of their own species, show interest, greet one another, often sniff one another's private areas. We're not suggesting anyone start *that* trend, but we are suggesting that the world would be a better place if people would start showing interest and feeling compassion for other members of their species.

The following guidelines will help you not be seen as a douche bag in public, and they will make your private life flow along more smoothly as well. Some of these rules seem so patently obvious we can't believe how many people don't already follow them. Others might be more obscure, but trust us, they're important because they create just a little bit more good karma in our world, and all of us can use some of that.

STOP TALKING SO LOUD

Of COURSE your life is incredibly interesting. Of COURSE you're the most important person in the room. Of COURSE everyone cares about everything you have to say. Of COURSE YOU'RE COMPLETELY DELUSIONAL.

We're sorry that mommy didn't teach you the distinction between an "inside voice" and an "outside voice," but that's not our fault. The rule of thumb is that only your companions should be kept abreast of your fabulous life, not diners across the room who can't finish their son's bar mitzvah because of your loud, obnoxious self.

Unless you are trying to keep someone from stepping out in front of a taxicab, there's no need to TALK SO FREAKING LOUD.

UNWRITTEN RULE #141: One should always talk only loudly enough to be heard by one's companions.

AND WHILE YOU'RE AT IT, STOP LAUGHING SO LOUD

Nothing's that funny! Laughing that loudly will *not* get you into your new date's pants, cause your boss to look favorably upon a promotion for you, or actually make a stupid joke funny. It will, however, land you a special place in hell, a place where you will be forced for all eternity to watch mimes, British humor, and Jerry Lewis films.

Laughter should be a tonic that raises the spirits. It should not be a club that knocks down total strangers in your immediate area. No loud laughter ever sounds sincere. So, if you want people to think you're insincere or not very bright, just keep laughing like that.

UNWRITTEN RULE #142: One should never laugh too loudly.

PLEASE, YOU'RE MAKING EVERYONE ILL

When you kiss someone—especially for the first time—it's a very special, private moment that should be shared privately. Did we mention that this act should be *private*? As in, not in the middle of a restaurant, club, street, bus, subway car, grocery store, church (Ick! God and your dead grandmother will see!), public swimming pool, or idyllic meadow (unless it's private).

PDA, or public displays of affection, is generally unacceptable. Look, if the United States just helped win World War II and our fighting men have just returned to the good ol' US of A, then, sure, some PDA is fine. But if you're just overflowing with love for the first lady to kiss you since your mom, then share this private moment privately.

Otherwise, you risk an epidemic of public nausea and vomiting.

UNWRITTEN RULE #143: One should rarely, if ever, engage in public displays of affection.

YOU'RE NOT SIAMESE TWINS

The younger person is always presented to the older or more distinguished, but a gentleman is always presented to a lady, even though he is an old gentleman of great distinction and the lady a mere slip of a girl.

—EMILY POST

Chang and Eng Bunker, the original Siamese twins, were forced to sit on the same side of a restaurant booth. For that matter, one brother had to look askance as his brother had sex with his wife. You, however, are more fortunate.

You are not required to sit on the same side of the booth as your husband/wife/significant other, yet, there you are, sharing the seat just like Chang and Eng.

Possible signals you're sending include: A) We're in a new relationship, and we're just so gosh darn happy! (Everyone assumes you'll be broken up in a month.); B) We're having problems, so we're trying to rekindle our relationship (Everyone assumes you'll be broken up in a month); or C) We're not very smart (Everyone just assumes you're not very smart and doesn't care how long your relationship will last).

UNWRITTEN RULE #144: Couples should never sit on the same side of the booth in a restaurant.

CAN I JUST ORDER FOR YOU?

You're starving as you creep along in a "fast" food line. You realize that part of the problem is the employees who dropped out of school with dreams of a singing career and GEDs in their heads only to wind up on the fry crew during third shift.

You can forgive those folks. After all, if you treat them poorly, they might spit or blow snot into your food. It's much harder to forgive the line laggers.

These are the folks who wait in line for ten minutes only to spend another ten ordering their food. What the hell were they doing while they waited? Sending their thousandth asinine text of the day? Besides, it's a fast food place they've been to a thousand times. They *know* they're going to order the same thing they always do. They, apparently, just want to give others the illusion that they possess free will.

UNWRITTEN RULE #145: One should always order quickly when one gets to the counter of a fast food restaurant.

DON'T GET CUTE

"Can I get you anything else?" the hard-working waitress asks.

"Yeah," the customer replies. "A lottery ticket worth $20 million."

Har, har, har. Now, the waitress is forced to smile or laugh or else risk losing a tip, and—let's face it—the customer probably wasn't going to plop down more than a buck anyway because he just seems like that kind of guy.

Please, for the love of the service industry, don't offer cute responses to direct questions. You may have nothing better to do than to clog your arteries with overcooked pork, but your server is trying to help a half-dozen tables after getting only a few hours of sleep because management gave her a turnaround shift. Just be pleasant, and save the jokes for your family. They *have* to put up with you.

UNWRITTEN RULE #146: One should never offer "cute" replies to questions asked by members of the service industry.

DON'T SUCK

Nothing could be more ill-bred than to treat curtly
any overture made in spontaneous friendliness.
—EMILY POST

Slurping the detritus of spit and soda that congregates at the very bottom of your fast food soda cup is a faux pas to be avoided at all costs.

First of all, it makes a disgusting sound. Secondly, it reminds people of mucus. Most people don't want to think about mucus under any circumstances. Thirdly, it makes you sound like a total slob, and even if you *are* a total slob, do you really want others to think of you that way?

UNWRITTEN RULE #147: One should never slurp the remains of a soda through a straw.

JUST ORDER THE NUMBER THREE, DAMN IT!

The quintessential "picky eater" scene can be found in the 1989 romantic comedy, *When Harry Met Sally*. Soon after the eponymous title characters have met, they go to a diner. Harry just orders something random. Sally, however, spends five minutes customizing her order, totally confusing the poor, frazzled server in the process.

If you are over the age of three and are still a fussy eater, your parents went horribly wrong. They probably gave in too much to your whims, considering them "cute" or "charming." Here's a news flash, now that you're a grownup: Taking twenty minutes to order a simple meal in a restaurant is not cute or charming. It's annoying. It makes you look like an insensitive creep. Even your parents would be disgusted with you by now.

**UNWRITTEN RULE #148: One should
never be a picky eater in public.**

KEEP IT CLOSED

*No thoroughbred lady would ever refuse to shake any
hand that is honorable, not even the hand of a coal
heaver at the risk of her fresh white glove.*
—EMILY POST

Now, we *know* mommy and daddy taught you better. In fact, chewing with one's mouth closed is, like, Life 101. It's one of the first rules you're ever taught in your life. It's probably the first thing you're taught after you've left the spitting-up-Gerber stage of gourmandizing (if, in fact, you have).

We can't believe we have to tell anyone this, but we have witnessed many a diner chewing away, all the while showing off the mashed-up contents of his or her repast. That goes against all etiquette. It's uncivilized. Let's face it: It's just gross. Grow up!

UNWRITTEN RULE #149: One should always chew one's food with one's mouth closed.

STEP *AWAY* FROM THE CAR

The front door is fifteen steps away. We counted for you (we had doubts about your ability to do it). All you've got to do is step out of your car, take those fifteen steps, knock on the door, get your child/neighbor's child/carpool partner/other, and head back to the car.

But no. This is too much for you because you are a lazy piece of trailer trash for whom "bumpkin" is too kind a word (in fact, "douche" is too kind a word). Instead, even though it's not yet 7 A.M. and many people are bound to be asleep, you lay on the horn. If your rider doesn't open the door within ten seconds, you honk it again.

Could you *be* more inconsiderate? Well, yes. You probably could. Nonetheless, please try, instead, to be less inconsiderate. Other people are sleeping, dude. The front door, as noted previously, is only steps from your car. No one's going to jack your stereo, drive off in your piece-of-crap Chevy, or try to talk to you about Jesus during those fifteen steps. You're just being lazy. Get out of the damn car!

UNWRITTEN RULE #150: One should always get out of the car and go to the door when retrieving someone, rather than honk the horn.

MOMMY'S WIDDLE BABEE

New York's bad manners are often condemned and often very deservedly.
—EMILY POST

We're very sorry that none of your relationships resulted in marriage and that you no longer have the option of bearing biological children. That is sad. But we have news for you. That's a *poodle*. It's not a human child.

Poodles, in the wild (if they exist in the wild), do not wear sweaters. They do not wear little chapeaus. They don't have monograms because they don't have initials. They do not speak English, nor do they speak "baby talk."

We understand that, to you, Precious is your offspring. To the rest of us, he's (in addition to everything else, you've foisted gender issues upon Precious) a dog. He eats his own feces when you're not around. He has fleas that the latest advancements in anti-pest technology will never cure. And, worst of all, he's spoiled.

How the hell does a dog become spoiled? Wow. You actually *have* managed to give Precious human characteristics. Unfortunately, you've turned him into a navel-gazing douche bag. Give the rest of us a break. Stop treating your dog like your child. It's pathetic and sad.

UNWRITTEN RULE #151: One should always remember that pets are animals, not humans.

DON'T BE A PRICK

Retail and waitressing jobs are tough. The hours suck. They don't pay well. They rarely possess any hint of upward mobility. Most folks who work in the service industry are doing so because they've been laid off from a better-paying job or because they have no other options. Many of them, in fact, work more than one job just to take care of their kids and put a modicum of food on the table.

So why, for the love of all that's holy, unholy, and in between, do you feel the need to be rude to these folks? Because they made a mistake? Good thing you've never done that (ha, ha, ha). Because they didn't smile? You try working eight hours, sleeping for three, and then working another eight hours. Because you're a sad, pathetic loser who feels so little supremacy in your life that the only jollies you get consist of wielding some iota of control over a wage slave? Bingo!

UNWRITTEN RULE #152: One should always be polite and courteous to members of the service industry.

MOVE YOUR *!#%! CART!

Grocery store aisles are, apparently, designed to be just wide enough for two carts to pass one another, like the proverbial two ships in the night. When you add to the narrowness of each aisle the fact that supermarkets always stick "items you can't live without" in front of the shelves, well then, cooperation is a must.

Guess what? This is America. Screw cooperation! It's every man/woman/child for him/herself! *Your* cart's in *my* way. It's not the other way around. If I want to leave my cart angled in such a way that no one can get by me while I peruse all the options available to me thanks to the kind folks at Hamburger Helper, then *you'll just have to wait.*

This appears to be the thought process for all shoppers. If you ask someone, kindly, to move her cart, then she shoots you a dirty look. And, OMG, if you have the temerity to try to move someone's cart out of the way so that you can get to a sack of hot fries, then you'll be treated like you tried to molest someone's child.

Folks, just move your damn cart out of the way of traffic. It's simple. Then, you can take as much time as you like price comparing or looking at MSG levels or counting calories or whatever the flip it is you're doing that's causing you to hold up everyone else.

UNWRITTEN RULE #153: One should always move one's cart out of the aisle in the grocery store when one has stopped moving one's cart.

A FAREWELL TO ARM(RESTS)

*You cannot commit a greater social blunder than to introduce,
to a person of position, someone she does not care to know.*

—EMILY POST

Flying sucks. Once upon a time it was cool. Now, in the age of terror and economic decline, it consists mostly of ultra-invasive airport screenings, payment for "amenities" that used to be free, and seats designed for Lilliputians.

Some things haven't changed, however. People are still acquisitive, avaricious a-holes when it comes to armrests. The only thing that's different is the battlefield territory is smaller.

No matter how you may try to justify it, you do not "deserve" both armrests. You fly a lot? So? Your miles don't entitle you to arm room. You're rich? Screw you, you cheap bastard! Next time, pay for first class where people still get treated like people rather than chattel.

Take one of the armrests, and leave the other for someone else. If you're on the aisle, then you get the one on the aisle. If you're at the window, you get the one by the window. And if you're the poor schmuck in the middle then—we've changed our minds—you deserve both armrests.

UNWRITTEN RULE #154: One should never be an armrest hog on an airplane (or other form of public transportation that includes armrests).

PROSELYTIZE SOMEWHERE ELSE

You love Jesus. You're fired up with the Holy Spirit. Well, hallelujah! Good for you! We are very glad you've got a first-class ticket to heaven, even though you used to be a drunk who shirked his responsibilities.

Be that as it may, we don't want to hear about it. Our own spiritual views are at least as important to us as yours are to you, or our own lack of spiritual views are equally important. This is America, and despite what some would like to believe, the country was founded as a haven for people of all faiths and for people of no faith. For that matter, we live in an increasingly multicultural country, one in which many people are God-fearing, though *not* Christian.

We understand that you are doing what you feel is your duty, but please stop. Be subtle. Leave a tract in a public bathroom. Put an appropriate bumper sticker on your car. But whatever you do, stay away from us and from our property.

UNWRITTEN RULE #155: One should not invade others' personal space by proselytizing.

CELL PHONES. MOVIE THEATER. 'NUFF SAID.

We hesitate to put this "unwritten rule" in our book because it shocks us that so many nematodes—disguised as human beings—still need to be told to shut off their goddamn cell phones when they go to the movies.

When your ring tone is on, it spoils suspense. And the killer is ... "All the single ladies. All the single ladies." Noooooooooooo! When you've got your phone on vibrate, you bug the living bejesus out of us every time you fish your phone out of your pocket or purse to reply to a text. Every time you put on your phone's display, you light up the room like it's a pop concert.

Once upon a time, people were not able to communicate at all times via an electronic device, and ... the world didn't come to a standstill. Individual lives rarely ever came to a standstill. People actually managed to wait until they left the theater to contact friends or loved ones and catch up on news.

There's no need to keep going on and on here. Turn off your phone, or, better yet, leave it in your car. Put your "busy" and "important" life on hold so that the rest of us can enjoy watching a movie, okay?

UNWRITTEN RULE #156: Turn off your cell phone and *don't touch it* while you're in a movie theater.

TALKING. MOVIE THEATER. 'NUFF SAID.

People do not greet each other in church, except at a wedding ...
It would be shocking to enter a church and hear a babel of voices!
—EMILY POST

Since 1927 or so, most motion pictures have included sound. That means these "talkies" feature dialogue in the midst of the action. We mention this because you seem unable to shut up during the film we're trying to enjoy. Your dialogue is not necessary. In fact, it's intrusive and rude. You, sir/madam/stupid-ass kid, are a rude, feckless jackass.

Talking, in general, is evil, but there is a special place in Hades for folks who let everyone else know what's about to happen because they've already seen the film. We wonder why they are moved to be human spoilers. Are they starved for attention? Are they basking in the fact that, for once in their lives, they know something others don't? Are they just discourteous d-bags? All of the above?

We don't know. We don't care. We just want them to know that, next time they open their stupid mouths in our vicinity, we intend to open up an industrial-strength can of whoop-ass on them.

UNWRITTEN RULE #157: One should keep one's mouth shut during a movie unless one sees that a fire has broken out in the theater.

PLEASE CURB YOUR CHILDREN

Ah, parenthood. The chance to do your part to ensure the future is brighter for the world. The chance to pass on a lifetime of knowledge to someone you love. The chance to piss off total strangers because your bratty kids are *screaming constantly in public!*

If you are one of those numbskulls who believes that children possess some sort of natural goodness—instead of possessing innate evil tendencies—and, therefore, you decline to discipline mewling little monsters in public, then please take our advice and never leave your freaking home for any reason.

Look, the only reason they throw temper tantrums when you're out and about is because you've taught them that losing one's shit publicly leads to rewards.

Tan their monstrous little hides once or twice the next time they have a tantrum at home, and they will be as good as gold forevermore. We're not advocating child abuse. We're merely imploring you to raise your children to understand that there are consequences for their actions and to understand that other people exist on the planet.

UNWRITTEN RULE #158: One should not allow one's children to engage in public meltdowns.

WATCH YOUR *!@%#
LANGUAGE, A##HOLE!

Elevated discourse has gone the way of the dodo, replaced by, ironically, dodos. At one time, people cared about the sensitivities of others. Even when angry at a friend or mate, they remained civil, especially in public, lest anyone hear unkind or coarse words.

These days, one will hear a gentleman walking down the street yelling into his cell phone at his "f'in' ho" who'd best stop it with her "fat-ass bitch self." And if that gentleman is using a Bluetooth, one might even believe these comments are directed *at* one. The fairer sex is no less prone to loutish language. They, too, speak of "ho's" and "bitches" who are "all up in their shit."

Should a family with small children walk by, these vulgar conversations don't stop. They may even get louder in the presence of others so that the speaker can better hear the responses of his/her "bitch-ass ho."

Real talk: This very public, very strident airing of grievances has to stop. While you're on the phone, you feel like you're in a cocoon, somehow not part of the space around you. Well, guess what, genius? You are, in fact, still among us. Our children hear you. Our moms hear you. *Stop.*

UNWRITTEN RULE #159: One should avoid loud cursing in public.

DON'T GRUNT AT THE GYM

Who does not dislike a "boneless" hand extended as though it were a spray of sea-weed or a miniature boiled pudding?
—EMILY POST

UGGGGHHHH! OOOOMMMMPPPPHHH! AHRGGGHHH!

These noises are *not* necessary when one is completing a set of clean and jerks (you jerk).

What is the point of this intrusive and irritating action? We can hear you *even with our headphones on, dude.* Okay, so you're a big, strong muscle man who could break us like a twig with the muscles in your nut sack. That's why we're taking the opportunity in this (distant) forum to tell you just how annoying everyone around you considers your constant caveman-like exhalations.

The ladies are not impressed. They're annoyed. They think you've got all the intelligence of a set of broken sporks. They fear getting involved with you and hearing those irritating noises in bed. We repeat: They are *not* impressed.

Other guys are equally irritated. They're just trying to get through their sets on the Nautilus equipment before they have to go in to work and be browbeaten by the boss. They're trying to attain a sort of Zen-like peace, but they can't freaking do it because you sound like you're about to give birth to a watermelon! Save the grunting for the toilet!

UNWRITTEN RULE #160: One should avoid excessive and loud grunting while lifting weights in the gym.

DON'T LEAVE THE EQUIPMENT SWEATY

One of the most disgusting things one can face publicly is butt sweat. What all is mixed up in that stuff? Dang, we just don't want to think about it. No one wants to face it. That's why we're puzzled. Why did you leave your ass drippings all over the seat of the abdominal crunch machine?

You can't help the fact that they got out, but then you walked away from the machine and went to another one. You missed one crucial step, you disgusting, uncouth piece of trailer trash: You forgot to wipe off the seat of the machine you just used.

No, you didn't. It just didn't occur to you to take the courteous step. You've done your three sets, so you don't need the ab cruncher any-more (actually, taking a look at you, you *do* need it, but that's another issue). Besides, if you go back for more, it's just your own booty juice on the seat, right?

UNWRITTEN RULE #161: One should always wipe down gym equipment after using it.

AVOID HARDCORE RINGTONES

Just because you think that Ben Folds' version of Dr. Dre's "Bitches Ain't Shit" is hilarious doesn't mean you should make that song your default ringtone. What if your grandma's around when you get a call? She might die, and we hate to inform you that she's already written you out of her will.

Don't get us wrong. It's perfectly acceptable to have a ringtone that's "you." Do you want to fool others into thinking you're intelligent? Let Beethoven announce callers. Do you want others to think you're "different"? Then use the Trashmen's "Surfin' Bird" as your ringtone. But there's no reason to choose a ringtone that announces you "go hard."

For one thing, you could cause an unpleasant incident in mixed company and, for another, anyone who uses a freaking *ringtone* to show he "go(es) hard" does not, in fact, go hard.

UNWRITTEN RULE #162: One should avoid ringtones that include cursing or other qualities others might consider inappropriate.

YOUR POOP DOES STINK

Lifting the hat is a conventional gesture of politeness shown to strangers only, not to be confused with bowing, which is a gesture used to acquaintances and friends.

—EMILY POST

Ugh. What's that smell? Nope. It's not that guy. Nope. It's not her. Nope. It's not even your boss. It's *you.*

Spiritual texts of all stripes point out it's never all right to do something bad just because someone else is doing it, or might be plotting to do it, or might be thinking about plotting to do it. The Bush Doctrine, the one that states it's okay to bomb the crap out of someone just because you think they might be planning to do the same to you? Only arguably okay on the world stage, and definitely not okay on a person-to-person basis. Pre-emptive acts of jerkiness are never justified.

If you couple your acts of petty terrorism with sentiments like, "I'm only doing what everyone else does" or "She did it to me first," then you're still an etiquette-lacking, pompous, selfish, uncouth bottom feeder. Your actions aren't any better, no matter how you may try to justify them.

UNWRITTEN RULE #163: One should always remember that one's own poop does, in fact, stink.

OH, BOY! WHAT?!? OH, CRAP!

All day you've been jonesin' for a Twinkie. All day at work, you picture the box. You see the smile of Twinkie the Kid, beckoning you to enjoy gooey, spongey goodness. Hell, you might even try to make a deep-fried Twinkie like they have at the fair.

Dang, those are tasty; and artery clogging and filled with enough calories to tranquilize a rhino, but so what? You've worked really hard today. For that matter, you've been pretty good with your diet of late. You've only snuck five or six cookies in the middle of the night instead of half the bag.

Finally, you're home. You look up in the cabinet and see the reassuring box. You start to deep fry some cooking oil. Once all systems are go, you proceed to retrieve some Twinkies only to find (dum, dum, *dum*) they're all gone. The box is there, but it's empty. Suddenly, you hate your life, your kids, your wife, your job, yourself.

Please, roommates and family members, don't let this happen to a loved one. Always throw away the box when you've emptied it so as not to bring up anyone's hopes.

UNWRITTEN RULE #164: One should always throw away a box once it is empty of food, rather than "trick" family members into thinking there actually are a few more Twinkies, cookies, etc.

YOU'RE NUTTIER THAN A FRUITCAKE

Nothing is so easy for any woman to acquire as a charming bow. It is such a short and fleeting duty.
—EMILY POST

Happy Holidays! We just wanted to say we don't really care all that much about you with this thoughtless gift: a freaking fruitcake *or* something purchased at the dollar store *or* something obviously re-gifted from last Christmas *or* (insert thoughtless "gift" here).

The most honest of all clichés—after "Life's a bitch and then you die"—is "It's the thought that counts." One reason human beings are considered more highly developed than, say, monkeys or dolphins, is because we have built-in bullshit detectors. We *know* when you've bought (or found in your basement) something that means nothing to you to give to us, who also mean nothing to you.

Why you've chosen to buy/find and then give us something meaningless is a puzzle. Guilt? Why?!? What did you do that we don't know about?!? Obligation? Yep, it sure is great to feel like someone's obligation. The desire to be considered nice? We know better!

Look, next year, don't get us anything. Please. Or, if you must, get us a gift card to Starbucks or something.

UNWRITTEN RULE #165: One should only give meaningful gifts to others.

DON'T OVERSTAY YOUR WELCOME

Unless you've decided to put the whole "real life" thing on hold and crash in your parents' basement, then no one *has* to put up with you. If you're lucky, you have a friend or two who doesn't mind you visiting . . . at least until he or she remembers why he or she didn't spend too much time with you "back in the day."

Most likely, old friends will get sick of you after *at most* three days. You can try to assuage the situation and get a few more days out of them by cleaning up after yourself, not peeing on their sofa while in a drunken stupor, and paying for a meal or two (or at least some groceries).

Whatever you do, don't be a freeloader. Pretend you have some common decency. Show them you've grown up a little, that you're not the guy whose whole life was focused on getting "Pussy Will Ow!" out of the garage and onto the music charts.

UNWRITTEN RULE #166: One should never stay for very long with old friends lest these old friends stop being friends at all.

AT LEAST PRETEND TO LIKE A GIFT

Even though we abhor thoughtless, bullshit gifts (see Rule #165), we still believe you should act like you appreciate the thoughtless, bullshit gift. And if the present is a poor choice but clearly was intended to please you, then you should go bananas with joy.

Gift-buying is tough, and missteps are bound to happen. If you told your grandmother you like Screamo, and she buys you a CD of Perry Como, then smile from ear to ear, say "thank you," and then get rid of the damn thing the moment she's back in the home having her Depends changed.

Gratefulness is a virtue, and even faking it is a virtue.

UNWRITTEN RULE #167: One should always pretend to like an unwanted gift.

SAY "THANKS"

For one person to look directly at another and not acknowledge the other's bow is such a breach of civility that only an unforgivable misdemeanor can warrant the rebuke.

—EMILY POST

If you're a nice person (we know it's not likely, so we said "*if*"), then you perform kind acts for others without thought of reward. You hold open doors for others. You let other motorists pull out in front of you in traffic. You do your share of cleaning up the house.

Nonetheless, admit it. You *hate* it when people are thankless morons who act like it's your freaking job to do nice things for them. How much effort does it take for a driver to give you the "thank-you wave" when you've let him out into traffic? "Thank you" is *two goddamn words*. Why can't some people seem to say them?!?

You: keep doing the nice things you do, regardless of how ungrateful others act. Others: stop being uncouth trailer trash and say, "thank you." Hell, you don't even have to go to *that* much effort. You can just shorten your gratitude to one word: *thanks.*

UNWRITTEN RULE #168: One should always say "thank you" when someone else does something nice.

WRITE THANKS

We understand that thank-you notes are like rotary dial telephones. They still exist, but they are rarely used except by one's great-grandmother (the one for whom dementia has not yet set in). This, however, does not excuse you from showing gratitude for exceptional acts of kindness.

You can go to your nearest dollar store and pick up a box of blank cards. Simply write, "Thanks for your thoughtful gift." Then mail the damn thing. It won't take you very long, and you will increase your karmic bank account exponentially.

If a note is just too much like work, then at least e-mail your thanks. Nearly everyone's got e-mail, probably even the aforementioned great-grandmother. Just put "Thank you" in the subject line, write a sentence or two, send, and *bam*: Good deed accomplished.

UNWRITTEN RULE #169: One should always write a thank-you note or e-mail when one receives a gift or is the recipient of an exceptionally kind gesture.

RESPOND TO CHEERY "GOOD MORNINGS"

You don't do mornings. We get that. You haven't had coffee yet or quietly masturbated in the bathroom yet or done whatever it is you do to wake yourself up. You hate so-called "morning people." You think they are scum who should be terminated immediately.

Nonetheless, you must find it in your heart to respond to cheery "good mornings" tossed your way by those insufferable morning people. They're just being nice. They just want a smiling face and kind words to greet you in your state of half-awake funk.

When you ignore a "good morning," you hurt the feelings of others. You distribute some of your pain on the undeserving. In short, you're a flaming prick (flaming pricks can be either gender, by the way).

We're not saying you have to engage the good-morning-er in witty banter. We're not asking you to wake up as Oscar Wilde, Dorothy Parker, or George Bernard Shaw. Just say "good morning" back. And maybe even try to smile a little.

UNWRITTEN RULE #170: One should always respond in kind to cheerful "good mornings."

DON'T TALK IN THE MEN'S ROOM

Do not attract attention to yourself in public. This is one of the fundamental rules of good breeding.

—EMILY POST

We find it hard to believe that some men didn't get the memo on this important aspect of public restroom etiquette. Nonetheless, as a public service, we feel we should bring to your attention this indisputable fact: Men do not like other men talking to them when they are standing up at a urinal.

We do not believe it has anything to do with bias against (or for) homosexuality. It just . . . well, dude, it just weirds us out. We're taking care of some important, and intimate, business, and there you are yapping at us while your mini apparatus dangles down.

Maybe you are descended from dogs, but *we don't like it.* So, please stop. Conversation and urination don't mix. Hold that thought until you're done holding your junk.

UNWRITTEN RULE #171: A gentleman should never try to engage another gentleman in conversation while both gentlemen are using urinals.

DON'T USE THE NEAREST URINAL

Hand in hand (that sounds dirty in the context) with not talking to others while in the men's room is this unwritten rule: Never use the urinal directly adjacent to someone else unless there is no other option. Sometimes when you gotta go, you gotta go where you gotta go.

If you're at a basketball game, then chances are you'll have to stand pretty close to other fellas at the piss trough. If the movie just let out and you want to hit the head before piling everyone into the car, then you will probably be standing up and doing business right next to someone else.

If, however, the washroom is mostly empty, then you should get as far away as possible from any other occupied urinal. Otherwise, you run the risk of creeping people out and having them think you're a psycho.

We have, however, heard of businesses at which the boss makes a *habit* of peeing right next to one of his employees in a sort-of literal pissing match. We're sorry, Mr. CEO, but you're just one sick bastard. You shouldn't have to go to that much trouble to show underlings that you're the company's biggest swinging weenie.

UNWRITTEN RULE #172: A gentleman should never use a urinal adjacent to an occupied urinal unless there is no other option.

SHOW SOME RESPECT!

Yes, the elderly can be annoying. Let's just admit that right at the start. They tend to be slow. They drive atrociously. They tend to be slow. They often are demanding. They don't hear well, causing one to yell. They tend to be slow. They don't comprehend or care to use newfangled technologies. They seem like relics of a bygone time. And they tend to be slow.

Nonetheless, they *have* earned our respect. They have experienced things—shortages, "good" wars, unimaginable leaps in technology—that younger people haven't. They grew up in a time when civility was the rule, not the exception. And, yes, they grew up in a slower time—no interstates, no cell phones, no five million useless cable channels.

As much as you may just want to body check grandma out of the way (hey, she's not *your* grandma), put yourself in her worn-out shoes. She's lived a long life, probably raised many kids, endured indescribable sorrows, and now, if she wants to take her time in the canned vegetable aisle, well, geez, let her and don't make a big deal about it.

Give up your seat to her on the subway or bus. Smile at her. Treat her like a human being and not like an obstacle.

UNWRITTEN RULE #173: One should always respect one's elders.

DON'T LAUGH! YOU COULD BE NEXT!

Ideal conversation should be a matter of equal give and take, but too often it is all "take."
—EMILY POST

Let's say you hate Larry. That jackass always seems to get promoted or to sell his stocks just before recessions or to have perfect kids who perform flawlessly in school. His wife is a former Miss USA runner-up. Larry has the perfect life.

You, of course, do not. Consequently, you hate Larry. Oh sure, you pretend it's for some legitimate reason—his dog ate your cat, his kids always beat your kids at every organized sport—but in your spleen you know you suffer from jealousy.

One day, you hear that Larry's wife has left him. You find out that one of his "perfect" kids is spending time at the methadone clinic. You even discover that the reason Larry was so "lucky" with his investments was due to insider trading and he's likely to go to prison.

Gloat to yourself, if you must, but do *not* gloat publicly. Your life isn't impeccable either. Remember "Jaynee" from that topless bar? Larry turned out to be a schmuck, just like you. If you publicly toss about his dirty laundry, then you're just going to attract attention to yours. If you create enough bad karma, then you're sure to follow Larry into the pits of hell.

UNWRITTEN RULE #174: One should never laugh or gloat publicly over another's misfortune.

IF YOU'VE GOT IT, DON'T FLAUNT IT

People hate you if you're rich and make a big show of it. We're sorry. That's just the truth. Sure, you may be the stereotypical "poor little rich guy/girl" whose life is fraught with depressing episodes and broken dreams, but you will receive no sympathy from people who struggle just to get by.

If you've got money, keep it as quiet as possible. Drive a normal car, not a Bentley. If you've got a palatial home, leave it off the holiday cards you send to friends. Don't name drop or discuss the "horrific" times you've had during your many world travels to exotic locations. You remember venereal disease and mosquitoes. We think of how much we'd like the *chance* to be in an exotic locale battling v.d. and bloodsuckers.

Tip well. Quietly help out your friends. Use your status to do some good in this world. If, instead, you choose to make a big show of what you have and we don't, then, as noted previously, all of us will hate you.

UNWRITTEN RULE #175: One should never flaunt one's wealth.

DON'T PICK AND GRIN

We would like to leave out this particular rule, assuming that everyone already knows it. Unfortunately, if you've taken a good look around you—in stopped traffic, in restaurants, in shops, in generic public places—then you know why we are compelled to explain the perils of nose-picking (and, for that matter, ear-digging).

A nice, juicy booger can be impossible to resist. We understand. You can *feel* it. It's *right there*. You know that you can get it with just one good pick. Then, after taking a look at it to make sure it isn't cancerous or in the shape of the Virgin Mary or something, you can ... what? You can do the "scrape off on the bottom of your shoe" method. You can do the "rub fingers together until particles are too small to detect" method.

The bottom line is there's now evidence, and it must be disposed of. Sometimes, that's tricky. Besides, you're probably going to eat with those fingers or (shudder) shake hands using them. Jesus! What if there are still booger particles somewhere on your hand or fingers?

We're not saying you must always leave that gold in your nose. We're just suggesting that you dig out those nuggets in a bathroom stall, wipe off everything well, and then wash your hands. No matter how discrete you try to be in public, someone will see you digging away in your nostrils.

UNWRITTEN RULE #176: One should never pick one's nose in public.

I BEG YOUR PARDON

There is a simple rule, by which if one is a voluble chatterer . . . one can at least refrain from being a pest or a bore. And the rule is merely, to stop and think.

—EMILY POST

The United States has more than 300 million people in it, and unless you want to live in a nowhere state like Wyoming or Montana, then chances are you're going to find elbow room in short supply. As a result, many of us have the unfortunate tendency to look at other human beings as obstacles rather than as, well, other human beings.

People, apparently, have forgotten how to say these two simple phrases: "Excuse me" and "I beg your pardon." If the latter has too many syllables for you and taxes your limited cranial capacity, then opt for the former: two words, three syllables. Easy to say, yet so rarely heard these days.

If you're in the grocery store and someone is blocking the aisle with his cart, then say these magic words and see what happens. Most of the time, the "obstacle" will be shocked back into acknowledging the existence of other human beings, will move his cart, and will mutter "sorry."

Anyone who hears your kind words and refuses to move, on the other hand, is a douche bag. You are welcome to push on by said douche bag because that's the other great things about such niceties as "I beg your pardon" and "Excuse me." If you say them, you then can feel free to nudge (nudge, not *shove*) someone out of the way because you've uttered them.

UNWRITTEN RULE #177: One should make frequent use of the statements "Excuse me" and "I beg your pardon."

DON'T DIS YOUR "FRIENDS"

You have a lot of people who consider you a friend. We don't know how this happened either. Nonetheless, it appears to be true. One reason we find your large number of friends a shock is the way you treat some of them at parties.

You give them the "broad jump stare." In other words, as they stand there talking to you, you are looking over or around them for somebody "better" to come into the room. "Better" could mean someone in a position to give you a promotion, a girl with whom you haven't slept, or someone whose proximity to you could (with difficulty) make you look cool.

Even if the "little people" around you are not deemed significant, you shouldn't treat them like they're human waste. For one thing, it's just plain rude. Well, since you don't care so much about *that*, we should also note that positions are subject to change.

The annoying weasel in marketing could become the head of your department tomorrow, and he'll remember that you dissed him at a party. That young lady you've done and run will spread rumors about how you gave her v.d. or couldn't get it up or something. Don't add insult to injury and ignore her at a shindig.

UNWRITTEN RULE #178: One should never ignore or "blow off" acquaintances or friends at social gatherings.

DON'T SNAP

Waiting tables has to be among the worst jobs imaginable. Sure, tips are involved, but most people are cheap asses who won't leave 10 percent, much less 15 or 20. You're constantly kept busy. You get blamed for mistakes others make.

Bartending isn't much better. You've got dozens of people in various states of inebriation wanting to be served *right now*, and they get all huffy if you have to wait on someone else first.

Please don't make it worse on these folks by snapping your fingers at them to get their attention. Anyone who snaps his or her fingers at a member of the service industry is sending the message: I am your master. You are my bitch. Nobody wants to be anybody's bitch, and *you* of all people should know that because you are the bitch of many.

Maybe that's your problem. You want others to feel your pain. But that's just not right. You could try improving your own situation and making it better rather than attempting to pull someone else down to your level of abject misery.

UNWRITTEN RULE #179: One should snap at dogs and *never* at other people.

CLEAR YOUR EARS

Nearly all faults or mistakes in conversation are caused by not thinking.

—EMILY POST

Selfish people unite! You have only your headphones to don! Gone are tiny transistor radios! In their place are technological marvels that allow you to take all of your favorite music with you wherever you go! You no longer even need to *pretend* to belong to the rest of the human race!

And that's a problem. People of all ages walk around with earbuds that never leave their ears. They are unaware of their surroundings, and they sure as hell are unaware of other human beings.

Sure, we understand that your favorite music can lift you up after you've had a rotten day at work or argument 5,003 with your significant other, but we also understand that civility is declining.

That trend isn't going to change as long as many people spend most of their time in their own, portable fortresses of solitude. All we are saying is give silence and interaction a chance. More importantly, we're saying *remove* the goddamn earphones when you're, say, interacting with other people.

Don't do the supremely a-hole move of taking out one earbud just long enough to tell the guy at the counter that he gave you the wrong change before putting it back in your ear and forgetting his existence. Don't meet a friend and make it clear you're more interested in Lady Gaga than what he or she has to say.

UNWRITTEN RULE #180: One should remove one's earbuds from time to time, especially when one interacts with other human beings.

NOT AT THE COUNTER!

Wearing earbuds while standing in line at the grocery store, the library, or wherever is bad enough (see previous rule), but we pray fervently that God will smite you in your spot if thou shalt be in line and worse, at the counter, while carrying on a (most likely) pointless and trivial cell phone conversation.

Many establishments even have signs entreating customers to turn off their cell phones while in line, but what are they going to do? Pay extra money for BlackBerry bouncers? "Excuse me, sir," they'll say, as they pick up your sorry cell phone–conversing ass and guide you toward the door, "but you'll have to leave until you can interact with our employees outside the presence of that cellular phone device."

When you just can't keep yourself from continuing your asinine conversation, you are not only treating the person behind the counter like a robot, but you're probably slowing things down considerably for those in line behind you. In short, you're being exponentially rude, rude on steroids, rude to the n'th degree. Just put down the damn phone already!

UNWRITTEN RULE #181: One should never engage in cell phone conversations while one is in line at a business or agency.

DON'T BE A GERM FACTORY

The interior monologue of a thoughtless, careless, self-centered idiot: "Ah-choo! Kaff! Kaff! Oh, sorry, got a . . . ah-choo! . . . bit of a cold. Here, let me give you some of these . . . Cough! Cough! . . . germs. Yeah, there you go. It's not enough for me to suffer in seclusion. I really want you to . . . ah-choo! Share my misery. That's why I . . . *snort* . . . don't bother to cover my mouth when I . . . ah-choo, ah-choo . . . cough or sneeze. I was only kidding about wanting you to share my misery because I . . . cough, cough, cough . . . am not even thinking about you. In fact, I don't *want* you to get sick because then . . . a-choo . . . I'm no longer the center of attention. Still, I'm not going to cover my mouth when I cough or sneeze because . . . cough, cough . . . I'm really just focused on me right now, as usual. If you get sick, we'll . . . ah-choo . . . just call that collateral damage or something. Man! I need some Kleenex! Oh, I'll just use one of your T-shirts . . . *hack, hack, hack,* man, this is a bad one. You'll probably be getting it . . . ah-choo . . . soon since, you know, I think it's just bourgeois to put your . . . cough, cough . . . hand over your mouth when you cough. Tell you what, though. When you get sick . . . ah-choo . . . I'll just ignore you and act like it's no big deal. *Ah-choo!*"

UNWRITTEN RULE #182: For God's sake, one should cover one's mouth when one coughs or sneezes.

WILL YOU DO ME A FAVOR?

Oh my God, here he comes again. It's *that guy.* You know the one. He's always got his hand out, asking for . . . well, you name it. Sometimes it's money that you know you'll never see again. Sometimes it's to "borrow" something that he, of course, never subsequently returns. Sometimes he just wants to "vent" to you about his oh-so difficult life.

Yet, if you ever go to *him* with a problem or request for a favor, you know what to expect: nothing, *nada, rien, niente.* In fact, he'll act like you're imposing on him for even having the temerity to ask for a small loan and god forbid you ask him for *your* leafblower back.

Even Jesus Christ Himself would have called guys like this "a-holes." Granted, He might have whispered the word or mumbled it or even just thought it, but He would have expressed it, believe us. The moral of the story: Don't be *that guy*.

UNWRITTEN RULE #183: One should never be a "favor hog" who *never* returns favors him or herself.

CHAPTER 6

UNWRITTEN RULES

IN WRITTEN AND SPOKEN COMMUNICATION

Mammoth sections of Emily Post's seminal 1922 guide to good manners and etiquette were devoted to the fine art of communication. In other words, even before e-mail, smartphones, mp3s, and whatever else has been invented since this book went to press, human beings had difficulty communicating with one another.

God only knows how Post might respond to the glut of distractions that exist today. She would probably have an aneurysm each time she witnessed someone "having a conversation" with someone else, even as both parties texted away such hasty epistles as "Waz gud?" and "LMFAO." Post would shart herself or worse whenever she witnessed people "having conversations" with earbuds stuck firmly into their ears. And don't even get her started on all of the rudeness and incivility that so-called social networking sites have engendered.

The bottom line is that we need Ms. Post more than ever, but alas, she has gone to the afterlife, a place, presumably, with genuine conversation, no texting, and with "meat space" social networking the only option. We will try to take up the Post mantle and point out some—in many cases painfully obvious—unwritten rules you should be following in regard to written and spoken communication.

THEIR IS NO EXCUSE

Mispelling! Its annoying! Even if your not to bright, you can probly detect mispelled words after a wile, and then your going too look for them instead of reading that e-mail.

See what we mean?

Technology may have destroyed the art of epistles, real letters that cover real topics written on real stationery, but it has at least replaced that art with technology that allows us to be perfect spellers. You were still in high school at the age of 22? So what! With your computer's spell check, you can still come off like a Rhodes Scholar (if Rhodes Scholars spent their time writing e-mails about where to score bud, that is).

Nowadays, the only thing standing between you and flawlessly spelled e-mails is laziness. There's a reason almost all e-mail providers offer a spell check feature. Try it sometime.

UNWRITTEN RULE #184: One should always use spell check before delivering an e-mail or letter.

DON'T "SHOUT"

Since the 1990s, when e-mail began to become a popular form of communication, most people have understood that WRITING IN ALL CAPS IS AKIN TO SHOUTING AT SOMEONE. Nonetheless, many people still put that caps lock button on and type away.

Picture yourself: You're sitting at your computer contemplating holiday gifts for little Johnny. You go to check out customer reviews, and MOST OF THEM ARE SCREAMING AT YOU.

Dang! All you wanted was to know if that doll Johnny wants (he's an odd one, that little Johnny; he doesn't even call a doll an action figure like boys are supposed to do ... maybe you've got bigger issues than RUDE TYPISTS ... but we digress), the one that drinks and wets itself, causes stains on furniture, and now you're on the receiving end of ALL-CAPS ABUSE. There oughta be a rule!

UNWRITTEN RULE #185: One should never write an entire e-mail in all capital letters.

THOU SHALT NOT FLAME

The single biggest problem in communication
is the illusion that it has taken place.
—GEORGE BERNARD SHAW

The late comedian George Carlin once had a bit suggesting that the vitriol you feel for someone is inversely proportionate to their distance from you. In other words, it's easy to call someone an a-hole if they're on television or back at the office. It's something else entirely to insult someone who's standing ten feet away.

Unfortunately, many—especially many teens—have discovered the truth of Carlin's logic. They engage in "flaming" or vile, uncouth, etiquette-free messages on chat boards or comment sections of online articles. That way, they can appear tough online, even if, in person, they're Cowardly Lions. They go online, send out vituperative insults, and then duck and run when the focus of their ire shows up.

Flaming sucks. It's fascist. It's evil. It makes the "flamer" look like an unprincipled moron. If the Internet had been around during the time of Moses, we're pretty sure a reference to flaming would have been in there somewhere . . . probably replacing that redundant one about worshiping false idols (isn't that covered by "no other gods"?).

UNWRITTEN RULE #186: One should never flame, or send intensely abusive messages, on the Internet.

WTF ARE YOU TRYING TO SAY?

Everyone understands such textspeak as "LOL" and "WTF," and even grandpa understands "OMG." Some folks, however, use so many arcane abbreviations that they might as well be communicating via hieroglyphics.

We get it. You're a texting maestro and are incredibly with it. But . . . isn't the basic, underlying point of texting to communicate? If so, then you're doing a piss-poor job. We can't understand you, and we're irritated by showoffs.

You're akin to a drunken redneck who says, "Watch this!" just before setting an M-80 off in his back pocket and blowing off an ass cheek. Just speak English, okay?

UNWRITTEN RULE #187: One should avoid obscure textspeak when texting.

PARAGRAPHS AND PUNCTUATION ARE GOOD

Letters e-mails and blog posts that confront the reader with one great big block of text can only be made worse when the writer of said epistle eschews all punctuation as well and makes his or her communication into one big Faulknerian sentence that no one in his or her right mind would take the time to read for fear of falling asleep before getting to the end of the text even if there might be important information in the midst of the communication such as look out your hair is on fire or something like that so what's important is that when you write something and want it to be read you need to offer the reader an occasional paragraph break and stop trying to be postmodern and dropping or becoming creative!!!! with punctuation.

UNWRITTEN RULE #188: One should always divide lengthy letters, e-mails, and blog posts into paragraphs and be sure to use accurate punctuation.

PRAYING IN PUBLIC

It's great that you love Jesus, but do you have to sing praises to him in the middle of the Golden Corral? Others just want to gorge themselves and do their part to make the United States the world's most obese country. All that thanking and stuff is rude because not everyone shares your faith.

Yes, we understand that you believe you are "testifying" and hoping to lead agnostic calves to the golden trough of eternity, but didn't Jesus Himself say something about prayers in secret being better than those made out in the open? Oh, yeah! He did!

Here's Matthew 6:6, just in case you've forgotten it: "But thou, when thou prayest, enter into thy closet, and when thou hast shut thy door, pray to thy Father which is in secret; and thy Father which seeth in secret shall reward thee openly."

So, unless Jesus has given you special dispensation (and He hasn't, doofus), then keep your praying behind closed doors.

UNWRITTEN RULE #189: One should never pray openly in public unless one is in a house of worship.

MUMBLING IS STUPID AND RUDE

He who knows does not speak. He who speaks does not know.
—LAO TZU

Some annoying people cannot *turn down the volume*, while other—equally annoying—people have trouble getting the volume up loud enough.

If you are someone who is frequently asked to repeat yourself, then, unless you work in a convalescent home, chances are you're a mumbler. Yeah, yeah, we understand that you mumble because you lack confidence or because mommy and daddy yelled at you a lot when you were a kid or something, but you're a big boy/big girl now.

So, here's a news flash: People hate mumblers. We feel as though you are being manipulative with your tiny, little voice. You're forcing us to put you center stage longer than necessary just so that we can engage in basic conversation with you. Speak up, or shut up.

UNWRITTEN RULE #190: One should never mumble when one speaks to others.

EYE CONTACT IS A NECESSITY

You've got something to hide. You're lying. You're plotting. You're mentally disturbed. You lack confidence, so we can squash you like a bug.

These are the things people assume about you if you refuse to make eye contact during conversation. And even if you are lying, lacking confidence, or hiding something, do you really want to announce this to others? If you're mentally disturbed, then you can't control yourself, and we feel for you. We really do.

People expect eye contact when they speak to you. It's probably for some deep-rooted psychological reason, a reason we can't explain, but the fact is people are suspicious or downright hostile toward those who refuse to look them in the eye during verbal intercourse (or other types of intercourse, for that matter).

UNWRITTEN RULE #191: One should always make eye contact during conversation.

DON'T . . . WHAT? . . . INTERRUPT

The best thing you can do to prove to others that you are a self-centered, navel-gazing jerk is to interrupt them constantly. Sure, what you've got to say is important, but it's not *more* important than what others have to say, even though you probably believe it is.

There *are* reasons to interrupt others: They're on fire. A car is barreling toward them. A meteor is falling from the sky and headed right for them. Otherwise, *shut up already*.

Your brilliance can take a temporary back seat to that of other raconteurs. Even if you're *dying* to break in, just count backward by threes from one hundred until the other speaker is finished. Even if you aren't really listening, you'll at least appear to be. Thus, others will stop avoiding your presence.

UNWRITTEN RULE #192: One should never interrupt others.

LIKE . . . YOU KNOW

"I was, like, so upset."

No. Either you *were* upset, or you were *not* upset. You were not "like" upset.

"It's just, like, so stupid, you know?"

No. We don't know. By making your statement into a question, you are trying to force us to agree with you about the situation, and, to be honest, we do not. Oh, and we'll just remind you that it either *is* so stupid or it is *not* so stupid. It's not "like" so stupid.

"Yeah, um, I um, think um, that . . ."

Tell you what. Get back to us when you've completed your thought. At this rate, it will be several minutes. We're going over to Starbucks for some grossly overpriced coffee. Repeatedly saying "um" makes you sound, like, so stupid, you know?

UNWRITTEN RULE #193: One should avoid such verbal "placeholders" as "like," "you know," and "um."

GUM-POPPING IS FOR EIGHT-YEAR-OLDS

Chewing gum can be a good way to give yourself fresh breath prior to a meeting, a date, or a get-together with friends. Popping gum constantly during these *tête-à-têtes* is a good way to lose friends and alienate people (or, at work, to get yourself a demotion).

Chances are, if you're a "gum-popper," then it's a nervous tic, and you're not even aware that you're doing it. But trust us. Everyone else within a 100-yard radius is *very* aware that you're popping that gum like it's your job or like you're Violet Beauregarde, the Chiclet-snapping character in *Charlie and the Chocolate Factory*.

Leave the snapping, crackling, and popping to those little elves (or sprites or fairies or whatever they are) that live within boxes of Rice Krispies.

UNWRITTEN RULE #194: One should never snap one's gum or blow bubbles with gum while one is communicating with others.

TO BE FRANK . . .

The most important things are the hardest to say because words diminish them.
—STEPHEN KING

Well, "Frank," we hate to be the ones to tell you this, but phrases such as "to be frank," "to be honest," and the like should always be avoided.

Why? They suggest a linguistic intimacy, indicating that all you've said prior to your "frankness" has been dishonest. Plus, people often use phrases like these to say things that are inappropriate, racist, sexist, or discriminatory in some way. Then, after such inappropriate comments are made, the onus is on you to agree or—should you choose not to—to do verbal battle with some jerk-off you don't even know.

One should always be frank and earnest, honest and virtuous, and sometimes that means keeping your stupid opinions to your stupid self.

UNWRITTEN RULE #195: During communication, one should always avoid statements like "to be honest" or "to be frank."

OH, REALLY? WELL, ONE TIME I . . .

People who turn the gentle art of conversation into a brutal bout of one-upmanship are etiquette-lacking doofi (plural of "doofus").

While it's okay to bond with another by sharing similar stories, it is most decidedly *not okay* to feel that you have to have a *better* story every time. To wit: Someone shares with you a story about how she broke a knee while skiing. You, then, feel the need to talk about how you broke your back and came *this close* to being paralyzed on the slopes. Even if your story is true, you come off like an eight-year-old saying, "That's nothing. This one time . . ."

Most likely, if you engage in this sort of brinksmanship, you're doing it because either A) you're a self-centered jerk; or B) you're a self-confidence-lacking mouse eager to appear to have a roar. People do not cotton to either type.

UNWRITTEN RULE #196: One should never try to "one-up" another when sharing stories about misfortunes, exciting events in their lives, etc.

ONLY ARGUE WHEN YOU KNOW WHAT THE HELL YOU'RE TALKING ABOUT!

Have you ever noticed that some people are experts on everything? Have you also noticed that these people are called "douches"?

If you know what you're talking about, then, sure, you should offer your cogent insight. If, however, you glanced at an update running on the ticker under Fox News's talking heads and now feel that you have a Kissinger-like grasp of foreign diplomacy, then you probably should keep your big, fat, stupid mouth shut.

It's okay to be ignorant about some things. Hell, it's okay to be ignorant about most things . . . *if* you're willing to admit your ignorance and demonstrate a desire to be enlightened. People like to feel that they can impart wisdom, and, someday, you may have the chance to take center stage with your knowledge of, say, beer pong or the location of top-shelf strip clubs in your area. Doubtful . . . but it *could* happen.

Oh, and one final note. If you are a boss and pretend that you know about things you don't, then you should be aware that every single one of your employees makes fun of you behind your back (and probably has developed a spot-on imitation of you that is trotted out after hours at various bars).

UNWRITTEN RULE #197: One should never argue a point when one knows little to nothing about the point being made.

USING LANGUAGE DISCORRECTLY MAKES YOU SOUND STUPID

If we are strong, our strength will speak for itself.
If we are weak, words will be of no help.
—JOHN F. KENNEDY

We're not saying that George W. Bush is stupid. There is no way (at least we would like to believe this) that you can be completely empty-headed and be elected president of the United States (we'll forget about ineffectual wankers like Warren G. Harding and Benjamin Pierce).

Nonetheless, Bush is proof that, regardless (not irregardless, which is not a word and would be redundant if it *were* a word) of one's intellectual capacity, you come off like a total moron if you say things like "Internets" (no "s" required), "misunderestimate" (if you coin a stupid-sounding neologism like this one, then *yes*, we will underestimate you), and "Is our children learning?" (perhaps, *if* they understand subject-verb agreement).

In real life, even people without speech writers try to sound intelligent by using "big words" that either are used incorrectly or are just plain made up. Malapropisms are funny, but they turn you into a figure of ridicule. Coining new words *can* work. After all, Sarah Palin got some mileage out of the neologism "refudiate," but, overall, you should stick to using words you know (the ones with fewer than three syllables, for example).

UNWRITTEN RULE #198: One should never attempt to sound intelligent by using "big words" one does not know or, worse, coining words that have never existed and should never exist.

ONLY TALK DOWN TO LITTLE PEOPLE

You're smart. We get that. You've got advanced degrees from the finest schools. Good for you! We know one more thing about you as well. You're an intellectual bully. Like a big, dumb guy uses his fists to beat others you use your big, smart brain to beat others (in a metaphorical sense).

Both kinds of bullies deserve special places in hell. And both usually act the way they do because they are trying to compensate for perceived or (more likely) real inadequacies: an embarrassing family, a slutty past, not enough love from mommy, a tiny tallywhacker.

If you have a superhuman brain, use it as a force for good. You'll find that you like yourself better, and you'll find that other people stop thinking you're a conceited prick. It's a win-win!

UNWRITTEN RULE #199: One should never use one's intelligence to make others feel stupid.

LEARN TO MAKE STATEMENTS?

Men and women belong to different species, and communication between them is still in its infancy.
—BILL COSBY

Some people, perhaps lacking self-confidence or common sense, speak only in questions? You know, their voices rise at the end of every sentence? And after a while, you just want to kill them?

This particular trait is so annoying because we are trained to answer questions, but how do you answer questions that aren't really questions? The result when faced with an "inquisitioner" is that one is stymied, forced just to nod and smile or adopt quizzical looks.

Please, grow a pair. Try to mix up your verbal retinue with the occasional declarative or even imperative (!!) statement. People will stop trying to avoid you. Well, we can't promise that because speaking in interrogatives is probably only one of many annoying qualities you possess, but this one is pretty easy to get rid of.

UNWRITTEN RULE #200: One should not speak in constant interrogative statements.

IF YOU CAN'T LAUGH FOR REAL . . .

A braying horse laugh or a nose-clearing snort of a chortle is annoying under any circumstances, but when they are used falsely to stroke the boss's ego or to "impress" a potential lover, then they cross the line into the boondocks of bad etiquette.

Unless someone's bullshit detector is missing completely, he or she can tell the difference between real laughter and fake laughter. Everyone loves getting a genuine laugh when they make a *bon mot*, but *nobody* likes to receive fake chuckles. They're the equivalent of a sitcom laugh track, and the louder your fake laugh, the more you annoy those you might actually be trying to impress or please.

UNWRITTEN RULE #201: One should never engage in loud, false laughter.

VISUAL QUOTATION MARKS ARE IRRITATING

Since the start of the post-modern era, irony has become king. Sincerity is harder to find than a living progressive Republican. Some people use a tone that suggests everything they say is meant to be ironic. That, in itself, is annoying.

Much worse are those snooty eggheads and "hip" teens who adopt a visual aid for their constant use of irony—the dreaded "air quotes." The act of holding up one's hands, spread apart about body length, turning the first two fingers on each hand into quotation marks, and vigorously wriggling them up and down is a serious affront to decency and etiquette.

First of all, it suggests that you are not sincere. Secondly, it suggests you think your listener is too stupid to detect your use of irony. And third, constant use of air quotes is just freaking annoying. You do *not* come across as an "intellectual." You come across as a "jerk-off."

UNWRITTEN RULE #202: One should rarely, if ever, use air quotes.

JUST SAY, "GREAT. THANKS!"

The tongue is the only tool that gets sharper with use.
—WASHINGTON IRVING

"Hi, Janice! How are you today?"

"Oh, I'm really dreading that noon meeting with Global Widgets, and I think I'm coming down with a cold or, possibly, cancer. My boyfriend just left me, and I've maxed out my credit cards."

"I'm sorry I asked."

Most likely, the first person in this little exchange would be too nice to make that last statement, but we can assure you that's what she's thinking.

We agree that small talk can be annoying, and if you have a friendship with a coworker, then an honest answer seems appropriate. But if you barely know Stella from accounting, then you don't need to offer her the bones of an Edgar Allan Poe tale when asked simply, "How's it going?"

People who ask this question are just trying to be nice and establish a (minimal) connection with you. Just smile, make an appropriate response, and move along.

UNWRITTEN RULE #203: One should never answer a stranger honestly when asked a question such as, "How are you today?"

I CAN'T REMEMBER WHAT I E-MAILED TO BEGIN WITH!

Usually, when you respond to an e-mail, the original message is included. This is helpful because, if you're like most people, your inbox is inundated with constant requests, reminders, and rubbish.

For unknown reasons, some people respond but do *not* include the original message. If you're lucky, you'll remember what you initially wrote. If not, you've got to do detective work: "Let's see, is this the guy who wants to buy my used car, or is this someone connected with that 'adult services' ad on Craigslist? Is this the person I think I might have gone to school with? Dang it!"

When someone sends a particularly labyrinthine message without attaching the original, then you're really in a quandary. Most likely, you'll wind up having to go to the trouble of sorting through your "sent" box, finding your original note, and then piecing together all the necessary details.

We don't know why some people refuse to include original messages to their e-mail replies, but we do know they are rude, boorish morons.

UNWRITTEN RULE #204: One should always include the original message when responding to an e-mail.

THOU SHALT NOT
"THOU SHALT NOT" OTHERS

Who died and made you God? Nobody? Oh, really? Well, then, why do you feel qualified to pronounce judgment on others?

Everyone has foibles, bad habits, and dabbles in the seven deadlies from time to time. Yes, even *you*. In fact, your willingness to get up in everyone's business sends the message to others that you have more skeletons in your closet than the average sinner.

If you *are* impeccable in your behavior, then you're still not off the hook because you're being prideful about your perfect behavior. You're one of those little kids on the playground, always rushing off yelling, "I'm telling!" We hated you then, and we still hate you now. Just take care of your own business, and stay the hell out of ours.

UNWRITTEN RULE #205: One should never be "holier than thou."

DON'T BE A LAST-WORD HOARDER

By swallowing evil words unsaid, no one has ever harmed his stomach.
—WINSTON CHURCHILL

Some people cannot allow others to have the last word. It's just a thing with them. Whatever the topic, whatever the tone, they must complete the conversation. You hate them. You know you do. It's okay to admit it. We won't tell.

If you're one of these last-word hoarders, stop it. Just stop it right now. Your need to pronounce finality on every conversation is wrong. It proves you have no self-confidence. It indicates you're not very bright because truly intelligent people aren't needy about the last word in a conversation.

Force yourself to hold back. Hell, give someone encouragement for making a good point, and let him or her have the last word. The world will not end. You will not drop dead. You will find that people begin to like you for a change.

UNWRITTEN RULE #206: One should not always try to have the last word in a conversation.

TALKING AND TEXTING DON'T MIX

People are addicted to texting because they love instant communication, but, ironically, they can become so addicted to "instant communication" that they engage in it while talking to another living, breathing human being in their vicinity.

There's just something unseemly about ignoring a flesh-and-blood human being so that you can communicate with a machine via alphabet-soup twaddle: LOL, LMFAO, AFDN.

Step away from the damn BlackBerry! Let your Android talk to other robots. Pay attention to the actual person in front of you. Folks who "talk to you" while texting simultaneously are like those egregious a-holes who talk to you at a party while looking over your shoulder the entire time, just in case someone "better" comes along (see Rule #178). Please, do your part to bring civility into the digital age.

UNWRITTEN RULE #207: One should never text while talking to a "real" person.

WHATEVER

To speak and to speak well are two things.
A fool may talk, but a wise man speaks.
—BEN JONSON

It's number one! It's number one! In 2009 *and* 2010, a Marist College poll voted the word "whatever" the nation's most annoying word or phrase.

And no wonder! Why do we hate thee? Let us count the ways . . .

1. It's a word often used by sulky, disaffected teens (*are* there other types of teens?) instead of the words "fuck you," which would get most teens in big trouble.
2. It's a word that first entered the public consciousness via vapid "valley girl" speech, the same lingo that brought us "like," as in, "that's so, like, stupid."
3. It's a word that a-holes use to be dismissive when they know they've lost an argument.
4. It's used by itself, but it is *not* a sentence.
5. It's a word women use when they want men to guess what the hell it is they *really* want, since they won't actually tell him.
6. It's just a stupid, stupid, stupid word.

UNWRITTEN RULE #208: One should never use the word "whatever" as a single-word utterance.

AVOID CLICHÉS

We're only scratching the surface when we point out that clichés rain like cats and dogs from the lips and keyboards of most people. An occasional cliché is acceptable. These phrases and clauses became clichés because they are so apt or descriptive. You don't agree? Well, we're just sayin'.

Some of them don't make sense, of course. Sleep like a baby? Anyone who has had children laughs ruefully at this one. Pouring like piss out of a boot? Colorful, but . . . ewww. Whose boot? How did it get piss in it?

Avoid clichés when you can. They make you sound trite and uneducated. Try instead to coin new clichés. That way, when you make a clever statement and are asked, "Who said that?" you honestly can answer, "I did." And, by the way, please avoid pointing out to the publishers how often clichés have been used in this book. Thanks!

UNWRITTEN RULE #209: One should avoid using clichés in verbal and written speech.

RELATIONSHIP STATUS . . . WHAT?!?

Social networking sites typically have a tab that indicates one's relationship status, and sometimes, this tab can cause you problems. Don't get us wrong. Yours will just say "single" for the foreseeable future, but picture the following scenario.

You and your girlfriend just had a big fight. Or worse, as far as you know, everything's going swimmingly. You log on to Facebook and find you've received dozens of "condolences" pertaining to the end of your relationship? WTF?!?

You find that you can no longer view your girlfriend's profile. You look at her relationship status which, mere hours ago, indicated that you were in a relationship, but now it says she's single. It hits you: Holy shiznit! She broke up with you, all your mutual friends know it, and *you* don't even know it yet! Suck city!

Don't do this to someone, okay? At least inform the dump-ee that you intend to dump him or her *before* posting this information on your profile.

UNWRITTEN RULE #210: One should never change one's relationship status on a social networking site without first informing one's newly minted "ex" that he or she is history.

POST NO PRIVATE GRIEVANCES PUBLICLY

Most conversations are simply monologues delivered in the presence of a witness.
—MARGARET MILLAR, AUTHOR

Someone has just royally pissed you off, and you've figured out the best way to deal with it. You'll go to the person, talk things over calmly, and settle your grievances like mature adults. Ha, ha, ha! Just kidding! We're talking about *you*. Nah, your great plan is to create the nastiest, meanest, foulest Facebook post your devious little (emphasis on "little") mind can generate.

After you've created your magnum opus, you have let the entire world know that so and so is a bleeping mother-bleeper who eats dog poop, wets the bed, and has sexual fantasies about his mama. Doesn't that feel good?

We hope not. Airing your grievances semi-publicly is rude, crass, uncool, and downright chickenshit. Chances are, if you see the mother-bleeper in public, you wouldn't say such mean things to his face and not just because you know he'd kick your mother-bleeping ass. You wouldn't do it because it's too personal and just too rude.

Just because you feel "safe" talking trash over the Internet doesn't make it any wiser a move. Some things are better left unsaid *and* unwritten.

UNWRITTEN RULE #211: One should never write nasty things on a social networking site about someone with whom one has a grievance.

DON'T BE STANDOFFISH

When you were a sullen, disaffected teen, the whole standoffish thing may have worked for you. Adults didn't really expect you to talk, and your friends probably thought your sullen attitude bespoke secret knowledge, world-weariness, and an interesting personality bubbling just under your Goth-draped surface.

You fooled them, didn't you? In fact, you were just shy and frightened of rejection. That's why you never opened your mouth.

Now that you're an adult, we have bad news for you. People tend to interpret standoffishness not as shyness but as douche-bag-iness. You'll *still* come across as sullen and disaffected, but you no longer have the "out" of being too young to attract notice.

Consequently, when you are in public—an office party or some other social occasion, for example—you are no longer allowed to sit there with your lips sewn shut. Force yourself to talk. The easiest thing is to introduce yourself, gather information about someone else, and then let him or her talk about himself or herself.

You'll discover that other people will reject you only if they sense that you don't like them. And how do you show that you don't like them? That's right! You sit there and say nothing.

Talk. Smile. It's easier than you think.

UNWRITTEN RULE #212: One should never be standoffish during social gatherings, no matter how shy one might be.

CAREFUL CONVERSATION

You're a card-carrying liberal, and you don't care who knows it. When you meet someone, well, damn the torpedoes, you're going to get across your political points and do your best to demolish those who espouse opposing views. You're honest, no bull. Straight talk. Real talk.

Well, guess what, jackass? You're being, well, a jackass.

Polite conversation isn't designed to alienate total strangers. It's designed to promote community, harmony, and understanding. If you leap right into hot-button topics, then you may get some lively debate as a result, but you will also garner a reputation as an ill-mannered, impolite, indecorous bonehead. You might even hurt someone else's feelings, and, despite what you may believe, this is *not* acceptable in the battle to further your truth crusade.

Back off. Once you've established a connection with someone, then you can consider sharing your views. If things heat up, cool them off by moving on to another topic.

UNWRITTEN RULE #213: One should avoid bringing up hot-button issues during initial conversations with strangers.

RECONNECT CAREFULLY

Talking is like playing on the harp; there is as much in laying the hands on the strings to stop their vibration as in twanging them to bring out their music.

—OLIVER WENDELL HOLMES

Reconnecting with old friends on social networking sites like Facebook is cool, no doubt. It's interesting to find out that "partying guy" is now a conservative Christian and father of three "perfect" and "beautiful" children.

Sometimes we can forget that people change from far left to far right in the course of a few years or decades. To us, old friends are stuck in amber like dinosaur poop. We don't know that, since high school or college, they hit rock bottom, became addicted to prescription cough syrup, caused an accident that maimed a toddler, and then magically "found" Jesus (He always seems to be lost.).

Consequently, you need to check your old friends' profiles before you decide to put something on a one-time buddy's/girlfriend's/boyfriend's wall that reflects them *then* rather than *now*. If you don't do this, you could get your old pal/flame in big trouble or, shit, cause them to relapse and maim another toddler. Do you really want a maimed toddler on your hands?!?

UNWRITTEN RULE #214: One should always check an old friend's profile on Facebook before putting something of questionable taste on his or her wall in case he or she has changed significantly over the years.

SOCIAL NETWORKING, NOT JOB NETWORKING

Networking in an effort to get job leads is fine, as long as you're not doing this in the guise of friendship. Facebook is for people trying to connect with real people in a virtual environment so that they can interact with these people solely on *their* terms. It's also for horny, divorced, middle-age guys who hope they can "reconnect" with high school sweethearts who have themselves become divorced and horny.

Facebook is *not*, however, for people trying to get jobs. Networking sites, such as LinkedIn, exist for people desperate to find work. We repeat: Facebook is for people who are just plain desperate. If you make "friends" with someone on Facebook just so you can use him/her as a prospective contact or as a reference, then you're what is commonly referred to as a *douche bag*.

Please, don't get up the hopes of horny middle-age men and women with your friend requests unless you're actually looking for semi-anonymous sex.

UNWRITTEN RULE #215: One should never treat a *social* networking site as a *career* networking site.

TAG! YOU'RE (NOT) IT!

People on Facebook love to post high school and childhood photos featuring some of their old friends with whom they've reconnected on the popular social network. One great way to *lose* those new/old friends is to tag them in unflattering pictures or to include mean-spirited captions or information in the guise of "jokes."

For example, if Barbra used to weigh 250 pounds and responded to (by crying, a lot of crying) the nickname "Rhino Ass," then you should probably *not* tag the grown-up Barbra with that unflattering name, especially since she now suffers from anorexia and bulimia. Now it's cruel on *at least* two levels.

In addition, that photo of Bob passed out drunk on the night of the prom is freaking awesome! Remember? You wrote on his face (in permanent marker, of course) such graffiti as, "I like to sux dix" and "Born to sux cox." Ha, ha, ha! But you probably shouldn't post the photo and tag him in it since he's now a Baptist minister and closeted homosexual.

UNWRITTEN RULE #216: One should not post embarrassing old photos that include "new" Facebook friends or post old photos that include "in" jokes that your now grown-up friend might consider in poor taste.

THAT'S SO GAY

*All noise is waste, so cultivate quietness in your speech, in
your thoughts, in your emotions. Speak habitually low.
Wait for attention, and then your low words
will be charged with dynamite.*
—ELBERT HUBBARD, WRITER AND PHILOSOPHER

Teens often say offensive things without even realizing they're doing it, and, to some extent, they can be forgiven. They're kids, and they don't know a damn thing. Adults, on the other hand, who make "unintentionally" derogatory slurs should just freaking know better.

Anyone who does not wish to be considered a racist, sexist, run-of-the-mill-discriminatory jerk-off should avoid saying any of the following things (or any of things *like* the following that are unintentionally left off):

- "That's so gay." Apparently, you mean that's just stupid or not cool. Instead, you're suggesting that people who *are* gay are stupid or not cool or otherwise defective.
- "That's very white of you." You'll still sometimes hear this chestnut, which suggests that only white people know how to behave properly.
- "I had to Jew him down on the price." Do we really need to explain why this is inappropriate?
- "My nigga." Black folks really shouldn't say this. White people *really, really* shouldn't say this. Ever.
- "I'm going to make him my bitch." Sigh. Calling someone one's "bitch" is just wrong on so many levels.

- "He's an Indian giver." Really? Listen, dude. Native Americans gave up—by force—everything we now think of as the United States. How did this expression ever come to be in the first place? It suggests someone gives then takes away. Um, wasn't it the federal government that did this *to* the Indians?

UNWRITTEN RULE #217: One should avoid making derogatory, discriminatory comments, even those that seem "harmless."

AS GOD IS MY WITNESS

"First, I want to thank God."

Wait, wait. You think that God spent any portion of His/Her/Its time focused on your music recording/film role/athletic performance? Is *that* why so many children starved to death and died of disease in Haiti? Because God was busy making sure you would win some award? He was otherwise occupied with *you* and your *entertainment product*?

Almost everyone can accept that famous people who thank God for their success should be forced to sweep the Augean stables for all eternity (i.e., shovel lots and lots of shit), but are they any less annoying than "just plain folks" who thank God *very publicly* for each and every "blessing" in *their* lives?

"Oh, God was looking out for us when I got this promotion."

No. He wasn't.

"Thank you, Jesus, for caring enough to make sure that storm avoided us."

Um, yeah, but it *didn't* avoid that town five miles away, and eleven people died. Did Jesus hate them?

We understand that you are just expressing your faith, and faith, in and of itself, is a good thing. However, next time you want to thank God *very publicly* for something, would you please think about how the "losers" feel? You know, the guy who got passed over so you could get that promotion? Or the families who lost their children in the storm that passed by your community?

UNWRITTEN RULE #218: One should keep one's thanks to a Higher Power private.

SEEMS TO BE THE HARDEST WORD

Two little words and so seldom heard: "I'm sorry." They're tough to say because they suggest that you have fucked up royally. Perhaps you hurt someone's feelings or took something that belonged to someone else or backed over someone's yappy dog (by accident ... yeah, by accident).

Men are noted for their inability to say these words (and for their masterful ability to screw up just about anything), but women often have trouble uttering them as well. Nonetheless, these words are necessary to keep the world (at least the civil world) moving.

That noted, be careful with the powerful words, "I'm sorry."

They are not, for example, to be used routinely when one makes the *same* mistake repeatedly. When they're uttered in that context, they really mean: "I'm not going to stop doing this thing that pisses you off because I really think you're wrong to be pissed off by it, or I actually think *you're* at fault." In other words, they actually do *not* acknowledge responsibility.

The words "I'm sorry" also should not be used after someone has done something really wrong . . . as in *evil*. The sentiment is hollow if a man utters, "I'm sorry," say, after hitting his wife/girlfriend/significant other. One should, obviously, not commit acts of atrocity at home, on the road, in the office, or anywhere else. But, if one does, one should not rely on "I'm sorry" uttered as an afterthought.

The bottom line is that "I'm sorry" is an important expression that *should* be uttered, but it should not be used inappropriately.

UNWRITTEN RULE #219: One should say, "I'm sorry," but one should also try to avoid acts that require one to be sorry.

CHAPTER 7

UNWRITTEN RULES

IN THE HOME, WITH SPECIAL ATTENTION TO WASHROOMS

Bathrooms are sacred sites in which some of life's most intimate acts occur. Often, these acts are unpleasant, though necessary. For example, vomiting one's way through a hangover is unpleasant, but boy does it make one feel better.

Washrooms are prone to all sorts of odiferous acts and opportunities for skirmishes of the sexes—seat up or down, bras and panties hanging or not hanging from the shower rod—and that is why following certain rules when one is taking care of business is so crucial to improving the quality of everyone's life.

While the bathroom is the site in one's house most likely to spread dissension and poor etiquette, it's by no means the only one prone to problems. What follows are rules for every room in the house, including non-sexual bedroom mores. For sex, see Chapters 3 and 4.

SHUT THE DOOR ALREADY!

You may think of yourself as an outdoorsman, rife with chest hair, who can take down a bull moose better than Sarah Palin, but you are not an animal. You were not born in a barn. Therefore, let us introduce you to the concept of modesty and sensitivity.

No one wants to come around the corner and see you standing—or worse, sitting . . . actually, maybe standing *is* worse (you know, your junk on display and all that)—above the toilet urinating like the proverbial race horse, a true denizen of barns.

There's a reason the bathroom has a door. It's so you can *close* it whenever you're doing your business inside.

UNWRITTEN RULE #220: One should always close the washroom door when one is going to the bathroom.

HOGS DO NOT BELONG IN THE *WASHROOM*

Road hogs are bad. Bathroom hogs are worse. In fact, they are among the most execrable of etiquette-deficient human beings. They should be forced to read Emily Post from cover to cover and then take a grueling test on its contents before being drawn and quartered by legions of toy poodles. And all of this should be done *while* the malefactor is suffering from the runs.

But we digress. Get in and get out should be thy motto.

UNWRITTEN RULE #221: One should always take as little time as possible in the washroom, regardless of how many washrooms might be available.

SEAT DOWN, MOFO

Women fought for the vote. Then they burned their bras. Then they fought for an equal rights amendment and, sorry, lost. Despite the women's empowerment movement, gentlemen, you still need to defer to the fairer sex when it comes to the porcelain throne.

What's that you say? "If they want to be treated as equals, then why do we have to put the seat down?"

Because you know you would like to get laid again during this decade. Because that's just the way it is. Because, until *you* have to deal with menstruation, carrying a baby for nine-plus months, lactating breasts, and a full-time job, you should just shut the hell up.

If your sense of fair play still feels bruised, then you're a jerk. Nonetheless, we have what might be an acceptable solution to the "problem" (it's not really a problem . . . you're just being lazy). Put down both seats. That's right. No more haggling and niggling and kvetching. Regardless of gender, some lifting is involved.

UNWRITTEN RULE #222: When one finishes urinating, one should put both seats down before washing one's hands.

LIFT THE SEAT, GENTLEMEN

If a visitor brings no maid of her own, the personal maid of the hostess (if she has one—otherwise the housemaid) always unpacks the bags or trunks [and] lays toilet articles out on the dressing-table and in the bathroom.

—EMILY POST

Drunkenness is no excuse for boorish behavior. Sure, when you've got to void four cheap beers after waiting—politely of course—in the line outside the bathroom, you're in a hurry to recycle those brews. Nonetheless, gentlemen, you must remember this cardinal rule: Pee over porcelain, not over wood or one of those doily-seat-cover-thingies (on second thought, screw those doily covers; feel free to drain the liz all over them).

No matter how careful you may try to be, you are likely to leave a few telltale drips on the seat, which would be most unappreciated by the young lady equally eager to rid herself of her wine coolers. If she sits in your careless puddle, then your odds of scoring are zero.

UNWRITTEN RULE #223: A gentleman should always lift the lid *and* the seat before voiding his bladder.

REPLACE THAT ROLL

Ah. There. All done. You've finally rid yourself of the remains of that super chimichanga with volcano sauce, and now you're ready to go out and commit further acts of gustatory sin. But wait! Egads, what's this?!? You reach over to get a few sheets of quilted toilet paper, and the roll is empty or inhabited only by the scraggly final portions of the once-hefty roll!

What should you do? First, you try to piece together a substantial amount of asswipe from those scraggly portions. But wait—as they say on commercials for stupid products—there's more (nasty stuff attached to your sphincter and not-so-downy cheeks). Do you sacrifice a wash-cloth? Is there even a washcloth available? Do you improvise a bidet? Do you sacrifice your underwear (it's already stained anyway)? Do you just pull up your pants and hope for the best?

If you're fortunate, there will be a stack of TP somewhere in the vicinity of the toilet. Otherwise, choose from among the best of the worst possible solutions.

UNWRITTEN RULE #224: One must always replace the toilet paper when one uses the last of the roll.

MERCY! FLUSH THAT THING

After you've done your grungiest business, the stink soon follows. Sometimes the smell and the, um, physical evidence are simultaneous. If you allow this unholy mix to gain strength, then you can turn a bathroom into a gas mask–required area in seconds. Oh, the humanity! Oh, the olfactory!

Since you've probably eaten yet another in a series of TV dinners replete with dozens of non-nutritional ingredients and topped it off with a generous heaping of ass-blasting hot sauce, your effluvium is an eleven on the "Who Died in Here?" scale. The faster the flush, the faster the bathroom can return to a state of harmony.

Try eating real food—fruit, nuts, berries—and maybe your stink will improve. Dang, can stink "improve"? In the meantime, please don't turn the bathroom into a chamber of horrors.

UNWRITTEN RULE #225: When one defecates, one should always flush instantly.

WHEN TWO FLUSHES JUST AREN'T ENOUGH

As few people care for more than one bath a day and many people prefer their bath before dinner instead of before breakfast, [having one's valet prepare a bath] is often performed at dinner dressing time instead of in the morning.

—EMILY POST

Sometimes, gastric distress can wreak havoc on one's innards, and the result, often, is a bowel movement of monumental proportions. And we're not just talking girth. What if you've left one of those explosive blasts, the type that leaves shrapnel all along the bowl, on the underside of the seat, and (gulp) sometimes even on the seat . . . the creeping filth, it calls for you!

First off, flush the toilet until most of the chunky mess is gone. Everyone knows your shit stinks, but they don't need to know that it's so ugly too. Folks just want to take a piss; they don't want to become amateur biologists. (Is that a particle of corn within that mess? Might that be the remains of a corn dog?) Those with weak stomachs may be tempted to blow chunks of their own.

Next, do *not* leave poopy streaks everywhere so that the place resembles a crime scene in brown. Once those streaks harden, they're harder to get off than a frigid female whale. Take a moment and wipe up the disgusting mess. Look for some all-purpose cleaner so that you can do a good cleaning job. If you leave that stuff all over the place, then you've just added an, ahem, shitload to your negative karmic debt.

UNWRITTEN RULE #226: If you have a particularly nasty bowel movement, then remove all traces of it from the toilet.

GET THE FILTH OFF YOUR HANDS

Even if you're absolutely certain that no urine was transferred onto your hands during the shaking (gentlemen) or wiping (ladies) process, you should wash your hands anyway. It doesn't matter that you don't intend afterward to perform surgery or cook a four-course meal; not washing your hands is just, well, icky, all right?

Microscopic poop is still poop. It lives on your hands then gets transferred to your food. That's why the United States keeps having e. coli outbreaks: Folks who pick the food that shows up in hoity toity grocery stores pop a squat then keep picking those alfalfa sprouts with pooh-pooh hands. There oughta be a law! Oh, wait. There *is* one.

Anyway, the whole "wash your hands, doofus" policy isn't even an unwritten rule in many public washrooms. Most restaurants, gas stations, and porn shops (so we've heard) have an official document from the state that exhorts employees (and by extension, everyone) to wash their hands. Often these commands are bilingual, so you can't possibly misinterpret them.

And, we hesitate even to mention this, but it goes without saying that defecation and hand-washing go together like peanut butter and jelly. Actually, on second thought . . . That's a gross comparison. Just do it, okay?

UNWRITTEN RULE #227: One must always wash one's hands after visiting the toilet.

DON'T BE A HOT WATER HOG

A comforting adjunct to a bathroom that is given to a woman is a hot water bottle with a woolen cover, hanging on the back of the door.
—EMILY POST

If you haven't paid attention to an earlier rule—keeping your time in the bathroom to a minimum—then shame on you. Already you have revealed yourself a probable finalist for the White Trash Olympics. Go ahead and buy yourself a twelve pack of cheap beer and prepare for the projectile vomiting contest. We're sure you'll be a finalist! (At least you're good at *something*.)

Leave some hot water for anyone else who might need a shower. How would you feel if you turned on the taps and had to take a cold shower? We're sure you already have had plenty of experience with cold showers.

UNWRITTEN RULE #228: One should never use up all of the hot water when taking a shower.

DRIPPING DRY IS A DRAG

Perhaps only learning that you have to get a pap smear (ladies) or a colonoscopy (gentlemen) can produce a sinking feeling worse than the one that accompanies emerging from the shower to find that there are no towels.

There you are: dripping wet, albeit very clean. Your eyes whirl about the bathroom. Toilet paper? No, that won't work. Paper towels? Perhaps, but you may have to use an entire roll. Finally, you settle on several washcloths. Then, you're late for work (again). You get fired. Yada yada yada. So, for want of a towel, your job is lost. Don't let this happen.

UNWRITTEN RULE #229: One should never take the last towel without replacing it with a new one.

OH, DRY UP!

Are you a fireman? No? Then why the hell are you dowsing the entire washroom? That curtain that hangs down from that metal rod thingy over the bathtub? It goes *inside* the tub, dumb ass.

If you have neglected to place the curtain properly, then the result is likely to be a flooded bathroom. That's just nasty. Who knows what all intimate bodily fluids may be mixed up in those tissues that missed the wastebasket and landed on the floor beside the shower? Dang, what if one of those nasty things brushes your ankle?

Also, water on the floor can compromise the structure of your home. One day, you'll get out onto the wet floor and fall right through to the basement. That would suck big time, and your family would hate your guts for destroying the bathroom (at least they'd hate you for a different reason this time). Bottom line: If you have flooded the bathroom, then make sure you wipe up the results.

UNWRITTEN RULE #230: One should not flood the bathroom while taking a shower, and if one does, then one should always dry up the resultant flood.

HAIRS BELONG ON YOUR CHINNY-CHIN-CHIN, NOT IN THE SINK

The housemaid does all the chamber work, cleans all silver on dressing-tables, polishes fixtures in the bathroom— in other words takes care of bedroom floors.

—EMILY POST

As a cultured gentleman, you, shave each day. However, many men finish their facial manscaping and leave the resulting detritus in the sink.

Dude, that is just unacceptable. Shaving cream and bristles in the sink? Nobody wants to see that. What if your mom came to visit? Although it makes one's morning ablutions take a few seconds more, one should always finish the task by cleaning up.

UNWRITTEN RULE #231: A gentleman always must rinse out the sink after he has completed the act of shaving.

THAT'S NOT YOUR RAZOR, MA'AM

Of course it's tempting, ladies. You don't shave every day like most gentlemen. Perhaps, your business attire allows you to go a week or more without shaving your legs, though we sternly frown upon this lazy approach to personal hygiene.

We, however, can overlook this *faux pas*. What we *cannot* condone, under any circumstances, is the misappropriation of a gentleman's razor. Seriously, ladies, that's just gross. Your leg hair clogs up the razor, which can lead the significant gentleman in your life to undergo a serious shaving incident: ingrown hairs, rashes, gashes. The mind reels.

Oh, and don't even get us started on the disgust factor related to shaving hairy pits with a purloined razor. Ewww.

UNWRITTEN RULE #232: A lady always uses her own razor, and does not appropriate the one used by the gentleman in her life, when shaving.

DON'T SQUEEZE ME, BRO

Toothpaste comes in a tube, which is a mistake. It should come in some sort of pump, like liquid soap, so that the perfect amount is distributed each time one brushes one's teeth—an act we suggest one engages in regularly. "Stank breath" is a definite etiquette *faux pas*.

Since the product does come in a tube, one always should squeeze it from the end to the opening. Otherwise, when someone tries to get some toothpaste, it's squeezed all the way to the back of the tube, wasting time, possibly causing a messy sink incident, and definitely causing the squeeze-ee to use inappropriate language—or worse—to leave without brushing his or her teeth and greet one with nuclear-level stank breath.

UNWRITTEN RULE #233: One should always squeeze toothpaste from the end of the tube to the opening of the tube and never squeeze from the middle of the tube.

PADS BE GONE

A bathroom should never (if avoidable)
be shared by a woman and a man.

—EMILY POST

Ladies, it should come as no surprise that most gentlemen are, well, just plain terrified of your monthly menstrual cycle. There's blood. You get cramps. Often, you get moody in ways that confuse and bewilder the men in your life.

Perhaps that—and the fact that most men have the maturity level of a precocious five-year-old girl—is why men get *completely freaked out* when they see a bloody Maxi Pad in the bathroom trash receptacle. Yes, gentlemen should just freaking grow up, but chances are, they won't. So, ladies, please. Put the pad where it won't be seen.

UNWRITTEN RULE #234: During one's menstrual cycle, one should dispose of one's Maxi Pads in places not visible to gentlemen.

DO WE HAVE A POLTERGEIST?
(LEAVING CABINETS OPEN)

There's a spooky scene early on in M. Night Shyamalan's one good movie, *The Sixth Sense*, that involves the kitchen. Cole's mother (Cole is the boy who can "see dead people"), Lynn, leaves her kitchen for an instant, only to turn around and find that every single drawer and cabinet in the kitchen is open. Well, she needn't have worried.

You see, some people have a serious problem. They can *open* a cabinet or drawer, but they have extreme difficulty *closing* said drawer or cabinet. The result is a kitchen that appears teeming with ghosts when, in fact, the spooky effect is just the result of mere mortal laziness.

The problem with these "human poltergeists" is that they create a potentially lethal (well, okay, not *lethal*, but damn painful) obstacle course, especially for those who might stumble into the kitchen in a sleepy daze. Picture it: Step, step, step, *bonk*! String of cursing. Blood dripping from gash in forehead.

Even sleepwalkers should be allowed to stagger through the kitchen without fear of gaping head wounds. Leave mysteriously open cabinets and drawers to the *real* poltergeists.

UNWRITTEN RULE #235: One should always close the drawers and cabinets one opens.

CONCRETE PLATES

Didn't mommy teach you better? Damn, dude, just putting your crumb-, juice-, gravy-, whateveritis-covered plates and bowls in the sink will not magically cause them to be rinsed. The result is that all those mysterious leftover food particles will dry up and bond like super glue.

Since you probably never actually do the dishes—or you'd know this and not do it—let us give you a glimpse of what it's like for the poor schmuck or schmuckette who *does* face these concretized bowls and plates.

First, they will try simply rinsing them, but the result will be nil. Let's say the "solvent" in the bowl is oatmeal. Fuhgeddaboudit. A power washer won't remove that crap once it's dried (And why are you eating oatmeal anyway . . . worried about your bowel movements, are you?). So, the person in charge of kitchen detail will have to use soap and a scrubbing sponge, and even then, the results will be questionable.

Of course, he or she could just choose to put the bowl into the dishwasher as is, but the bowl will come out with particles of oatmeal still stuck to it like rust stains in a toilet tank. Look, next time, just rinse the damn plate/bowl/whatever, will ya?

UNWRITTEN RULE #236: One should always wash one's plates, bowls, pots, pans, silverware, etc. in a timely fashion rather than just leave it in the sink to fester.

FILL 'ER UP

Her manner to a duke who happens to be staying in the house is not a bit more courteous than her manner to the kitchen-maid whom she chances to meet in the kitchen gardens whither she has gone with the children to see the new kittens.

—EMILY POST

Folks who have had lazy roommates (or folks who *are* lazy roommates) will be familiar with the chronic, misfortunate condition of the vastly underserved dishwasher. You know, you open the dishwasher and find that an entire load has been run . . . for one fork and two plates.

When only a few items are washed, the angels cry. They hate to see water wasted. They tear up at the thought of exorbitant water bills resulting from underserved dishwashers. They inform Santa, who puts offenders on the naughty list, leaving them—not coal—but dishwashing detergent in their stockings.

If you are too lazy to wash a couple of plates and a fork, then you are too lazy to live. You probably begrudge your lungs and heart for all that constant activity (at least your brain spends a lot of time resting). If you are too impatient to wait for the dishwasher to fill up before running it, then you are too impatient to live. One of these days you'll fall down an elevator shaft because you're too impatient to notice that there's been a glitch and there's no car. When that happens, we will weep, but first, we will laugh.

UNWRITTEN RULE #237: One should never run the dishwasher until it actually is full and needs to be run.

I'VE GOT DIBS ON PAPA SMURF

If you've got several people living under your roof, then avoid ugly scenes like these:

1. Someone is drinking from a glass so filthy it looks like it was borrowed from the bowels of hell.

2. Someone is drinking from *your* glass, and that guy/gal is the one among you most likely to have an as-yet-undiagnosed social disease.
3. Someone is drinking water from the tap using cupped hands as a glass.
4. Someone is drinking juice/soda/whatever directly from the carton/bottle/whatever not because he (almost always a "he") typically does this but because he feels he has no other choice.
5. Someone is drinking something out of your commemorative beer stein that is never, ever, ever actually to be used as a drinking device. *It's for show.*

These scenes, and others like them, occur when no clean glasses are available. Why aren't there any available? Because folks aren't using the same ones more than once.

If the tumblers all look the same, get a Sharpie and write names on them. If all you have is mismatched stuff picked up from thrift stores, then all the better. Each person can choose the glass featuring his or her favorite cartoon character or pithy saying and then use it repeatedly.

UNWRITTEN RULE #238: There is rarely any reason not to use the same glass more than once in order to ensure that your home doesn't run out of glasses.

GETTIN' SCRAPPY

It stands to reason that one may expect more perfect service from a "specialist" than from one whose functions are multiple.

—EMILY POST

You are a blue blood, a Rosenburg, of the Cleveland Rosenburgs. Your solidly middle-middle class home was replete with a garbage disposal. When you were finished moving all the food around on your plate in an effort to score dessert without actually eating much real food, all you had to do was dump the contents of your plate into the sink, flip a switch, and watch those asparagus stalks disappear into the nether regions of the city.

As a result of your pampered upbringing, you have developed the habit of believing that *every* home contains a garbage disposal. So, unlike your wife/girlfriend/roommates who know better, you dump the contents of your plate into the sink and walk off. You *should* know something's up because there's no switch to flip, but you don't care. Somehow, magically, the food you dumped in the sink disappears.

Well, guess what? It doesn't magically disappear. Your girlfriend/wife/roommate had to put his or her hands into your nasty scraps, remove them from the sink, and throw them into the trash can. That's just foul.

They're too nice to say anything, so we've elected to do it instead. You're gross, uncouth, and on a one way trip to Redneckville. It's not a nice place, bro. We've been there.

UNWRITTEN RULE #239: One should always dump one's scraps into the trash can (or compost bin!) if the sink does not have a garbage disposal.

PUT POP BACK

Dishes are never passed from hand to hand at a dinner, not even at the smallest and most informal one.

—EMILY POST

Some folks' mottos should be, "If it ain't worth doing half-assed, it ain't worth doing at all." Case in point: People who get a carton of milk or bottle of soda from the fridge, pour it into a glass (or, more likely, just drink straight out of the bottle or carton), and then . . . leave the container out on the counter.

The, to them, most important part of their job is done. Screw follow-through! It's not like they complete anything else (just ask their girlfriends). Now, due to their laziness and thoughtlessness, others will cry over spoiled milk and warm pop. Sure, you could put ice in it . . . if there were any ice.

That douche who left the soda out on the counter was the last to use the ice trays. The odds of him going to the trouble of refilling them are equivalent to the odds of Detroit producing a car that doesn't suck. Don't even bother to look. For some reason, the trays *are* in the freezer; they're just empty.

UNWRITTEN RULE #240: One should always put milk, soda, juice, etc., back into the refrigerator after use.

YOUR TOP ISN'T SHOWING

The parasitic twin of not putting beverages back into the refrigerator (see previous rule) is not putting the cap back on the soda tightly enough. What in the name of all that is wholesome, hearty, healthy, and holy is *that* about?

We don't claim to be scientists, but we do understand that carbonated beverages lose their carbonation quickly when the containers holding them aren't sealed. Hell, the "fizz" doesn't last all that long when the top *is* put on the soda. We also know something else: Soda lacking carbonation sucks. A guy lost in the desert who is rescued in the nick of time and given "flat" soda would drink it, sure, but then he'd put it down and say, "Thanks, but that stuff sucks."

How many gallons of pop have been wasted by inconsiderate schmucks who are too lazy to put the cap back on a soda bottle? You could probably take all of it and float a Princess Cruise Ship. Someone should organize a benefit: Pop Aid. Organizers wouldn't need to ask for money. They could just show tear-inducing shots of flat, topless soda bottles while playing a written-for-the-show anthem instructing everyone to stop being abject trailer trash and replace the damn tops already.

**UNWRITTEN RULE #241: One should always
replace the top on a large bottle of soda tightly
so that its contents will not go flat.**

PLEASE LET THEM DIE WITH DIGNITY

Wilted lettuce. Flaccid carrots. Carcasses of long-ago feasts. Gluten-free pudding (a failed experiment) that expired two years ago yet is kept on life-support within the darkened confines of a disgusted refrigerator.

Someone has got to step up, take responsibility, and be the one who throws out all the egregiously-past-its-expiration-date items in the refrigerator. Why don't you volunteer? Then, you'll see that your "stuffed" refrigerator actually is a columbarium containing the metaphorical ashes of food that wouldn't even be edible to a dog (and they eat their own poop).

If you live by yourself, then a refrigerator filled with outdated crap is just, well, sad, a reflection on your lonely, empty, joyless life. If you live in a house filled with people, then a refrigerator top heavy with the long-ago expired indicates laziness and an unhealthy lifestyle (all that crap is in there because you go out for double-stuffed burritos every night instead of, say, cooking).

Do yourself a favor. Free the fridge from the tyranny of the dead. Allow the corpses of vegetables and moldy leftovers (did you *really* think you'd go back for seconds?) to be buried in a landfill. Set their souls free so that they can gambol in the glens of leftover heaven.

UNWRITTEN RULE #242: One should always keep an eye on items in the refrigerator and dispose of them once they expire.

I DON'T EVEN WANT TO THINK ABOUT WHAT THAT IS

Just as no chain is stronger than its weakest link, no manners can be expected to stand a strain beyond their daily test at home.

—EMILY POST

Tonight on *Shock Theater . . . The Man Who Got Stuck to the Floor* (sounds of screams and moans, maybe some thunder, a lightning flash, etc.). *See* the roommate/husband/whoever look down in horror at the gummy, viscous substance on the kitchen floor! *Hear* his yells of surprise followed by strings of invective too horrifying to be reflected here!

Most people are willing to wipe up a spill when they cause one. That's usually easy enough, provided there are paper towels handy. What many people are *not* willing to do, however, is clean up spills properly when they're comprised of anything other than water.

You see, water contains no sugar or other additives that cause it to become a sticky, nearly invisible mess on the floor that remains long after the majority of the spill itself has been removed. Juice, soda, beer, pretty much anything else *does* contain stuff that is sticky.

That's why you need to clean up spills with paper towels *and* with some sort of all-purpose cleaner (assuming you have one). Otherwise, all you've done is your typical half-assed job (at least you excel at being half-assed . . . Take a bow!) that will cause problems for others.

UNWRITTEN RULE #243: One should always clean up potentially sticky spills with a paper towel *and* with an all-purpose cleaner.

REACH FOR THE DRY

Thank God! You've finally decided to wash some clothes. How long have you been wearing that T-shirt around the house? It's got to be at least since George W. Bush was still president. Had we invaded Iraq yet? And we don't even want to think about how rarely (ever?) you change your underwear. Just because you ignore the Hershey squirts or skid marks doesn't mean they aren't *there*.

We're proud of you. Really. But here's where our commendations end. Since you've made it clear that you are going to take care of the laundry, we don't think about it. Blissfully unaware, we go about our daily lives, waiting for freshly laundered vestments.

After a few days, we realize we've never seen these allegedly cleaned clothes. We can see that the laundry baskets are missing, so *something* must have been done. When we finally go to the laundry room to investigate we find (bum, bum, *bum*) you've left the clothes in the god-damn washing machine for three days.

Well, thanks, genius! By now they've started to mildew. In some cases, the smell will never come out, and some of our favorite articles of clothing will have to be thrown away. Christ, we should have known you couldn't handle a simple project like washing clothes. Now, you must die.

UNWRITTEN RULE #244: One should always remove clothing from the washing machine and put it into the dryer directly after the washing cycle ends.

WHEN LINT ATTACKS

**In the present day of rush and hurry,
there is little time for "home" example.**

—EMILY POST

We'll guess that you have no clue that a lint trap exists. It's this thingy inside the dryer that, well, collects lint, fibers, bits of paper with girls' numbers on them (don't worry, they're fake numbers, so you aren't missing anything), pieces of dryer sheets, etc.

It's the etc. that's kind of scary. What *is* that crap? Why is it always that sort-of mousy color? How many pieces of dead skin are in that lint? Is the dust of ancient civilizations trapped in there along with microscopic bits of semen-soaked sweatsocks (try wearing them instead of, um, *using* them next time)?

The bottom line is that the lint trap gets full, and quickly. If you don't remove the gunk, your dryer will get overheated and break down, causing you to be hated by your roommates/wives/girlfriends (yep, we're assuming you're a guy if you don't even know a lint trap exists) even more than you are presently.

UNWRITTEN RULE #245: One should always empty the lint trap after drying a load of clothes.

BLOOD, SWEAT, AND GOD ONLY KNOWS WHAT ELSE

Some folks just throw everything into the washing machine, assuming that the gods of cleanliness will take care of whatever mess they made. Unfortunately, the gods are little-g gods. They're not granted real superpowers.

If you got drunk, got into a fight, and (naturally) got your ass kicked, resulting in clothes covered with blood (just yours; you have to land a punch to get someone *else's* blood on you), then, please don't throw your disgusting bloody clothes into the washing machine, you needle-headed miscreant, you.

If you tried to do an oil change on your car in order to save a few bucks and (naturally) screwed it up, getting oil all over your clothes, then please don't strip off your clothes (definitely not around *us* anyway) and throw them straight into the washing machine, you block-headed reprobate, you.

In short (too late, yeah, heard that one before), if you've made an ungodly mess, then either throw your clothes away (you can always go back to Goodwill for more) or soak them, preferably not in the kitchen sink. Get a bucket or something, throw some detergent in it, and let your clothes soak until they've been de-nastied enough to be placed safely into the washing machine.

UNWRITTEN RULE #246: One should never throw extremely dirty clothing directly into the washing machine without soaking it, removing excess filth first.

FOLD, OR WE'LL FOLD YOU

If there's any household chore more fraught with half-assed peril than washing clothes, then we don't know what it is. By "half-assed peril," we mean opportunities to screw shit up royally if any of the steps are completed in a half-assed manner. And since many people believe no job should be done unless it can be done poorly (hey, this is America!), then odds are even that your clothes will never look and/or smell right.

One of the steps most often left half-assed is the post-dryer removal/fold. Often, someone will run the dryer and just leave the clothes sitting there, perhaps after grabbing (we hope) a clean pair of underwear. This is a bad move for two main reasons: The clothes might not have been fully dried, which will lead to mildew and bad smells. In addition, the longer the clothes remain in the dryer, the more wrinkled they will become, and since we *know* you won't bother to run an iron over them, then you'll be a rumpled mess at work.

Folding clothes is a freaking drag, no doubt. Nonetheless, nothing good will come of leaving possibly still wet clothes in the dryer for days, in hopes that someone else will go to the trouble of folding them (or at least removing them from the goddamn dryer).

UNWRITTEN RULE #247: One should never leave clothes in the dryer indefinitely.

DON'T BE INDISCRIMINATE

How many times has one heard someone say: "I won't dress for dinner—no one is coming in." Or, "That old dress will do!" Old clothes! No manners! And what is the result? One more wife wonders why her husband neglects her.

—EMILY POST

Look, dude, in your personal life, you can be as indiscriminate as you want. No one's going to sleep with you anyway, in your wrinkled, discolored clothes. See, that's the problem. You were indiscriminate in the laundry room, and now you're paying the price. Of course, your breath, looks, and personality aren't helping your love life either, but there's not much we can do about those issues.

We can, however, try to make you mindful of the perils of arbitrary laundry habits.

1. Washing stuff in hot *shrinks* it. Trust us, you don't need anything else to be smaller than it already is.
2. Washing colors with whites causes the colors to bleed onto the whites. You may be okay with pink athletic socks, but the other guys on your neighborhood rugby team will be ready to kick your ass (again).
3. Overloading the washing machine because you don't want to spend the time to do two loads could destroy the washing machine or keep your clothes from being cleaned adequately (and you *need* them cleaned adequately).

4. Directions like "dry clean only" or "wash only in gentle cycle" are not suggestions. If you ignore them, you will wreak havoc.

If you can start being more discerning in the laundry room, then you might stop looking like a total slob, and hence, finally get laid. At least you'll look good sitting alone in that singles bar.

UNWRITTEN RULE #248: One should follow washing directions and use common sense when doing the laundry.

REMOTE WARS!

Men typically want to feel that they are in charge, so they have a tendency to hoard remotes on their side of the couch. Besides, men have the irritating (to women) habit of changing channels constantly. This show is okay, but what if something *even better* is on another channel?

Women, understandably, do not like to be treated as the "second sex" when it comes to the remote. They want control of the ransomed remote, and they are seriously considering throwing a lamp at you if you don't stop *changing the goddamn channel*.

There's no simple solution to this problem. Some version of it probably occurred in caves during Cro-Magnon times. Og held the blackened cave-painting stick, constantly doodling on the walls, while Yona yelled at him to just pick one thing and freaking draw it already.

The best method with which to unravel this Gordian knot of an issue is to have designated remote control nights. Bob gets the damn thing on certain evenings, and Martha gets it on others. Disagreements may still pop up, but what else are you going to do? Hey, here's a thought! Turn off the idiot box and read or something. Stop killing your brain cells with mindless pap and suckling at the flat screen teat. Again, just a thought.

UNWRITTEN RULE #249: Couples should decide on a remote control-sharing method agreeable to both parties.

THEY CAN'T HEAR YOU

Some people suffer from a condition that would be pitiable if it weren't so goddamned annoying. They are compelled to respond to the television.

PUNDIT: Well, clearly, the political right is taking the high ground here and refusing to join in any name-calling or mud-slinging, so . . .

AFFLICTED PERSON: No! That's total bullshit! They're just trying to be seen as the good guys! It's the oldest trick in the book . . .

LOVED ONE WITH AFFLICTED PERSON: Honey, it's a television, not a live performance. They can't hear you.

AFFLICTED PERSON: I know. I know.

PUNDIT: Actually, I believe the left is making the best of this situation because we're refusing to let it sway us in our efforts . . .

AFFLICTED PERSON: Oh, for Christ's sake. You guys on the left have *no balls*. Of *course* you'll "be swayed," you a-hole!

LOVED ONE WITH AFFLICTED PERSON: Honey, it's a television, not a live performance. They can't hear you.

Etc.

Please, help the afflicted in your life. Give them a metaphorical knock-up-side the head the next time they refuse to acknowledge the fact that people on television cannot hear them.

UNWRITTEN RULE #250: One should never speak to the television as though the people on screen can hear one.

RING AROUND THE MORON

Glasses sweat, just like your smelly self. You get giant rings under your pits whenever you start to exercise because you're so out of shape. Likewise, a glass sitting on an object—like say an antique table (!!!)—will leave rings on that object.

That's why some genius long ago invented something called a *coaster*. A *coaster* is an object designed to catch the "sweat" from a glass or bottle. That way, the rings are left on the coaster and not on the antique table.

Unfortunately, many people seem to disregard coasters altogether, and that can ruin furniture. As a result, you may no longer be asked back to someone's house, and freeloaders like yourself can't afford to lose any more friends whose homes include copious amounts of free-flowing beer.

If there isn't a coaster, don't worry. Anything will do: a magazine subscription card, a piece of scrap paper, a chihuahua. Just be careful that you don't choose something valuable, such as a first edition of *The Making of Americans*, as your substitute coaster, and always ask first before actually placing drinks on top of chihuahuas.

UNWRITTEN RULE #251: One should always use a coaster. Always.

AFTERWORD

If you have completed reading this tome of modern mores, then what are you waiting for? It's time to put this (very polite—except when it's rude) advice into action.

Even if you never leave your home, you can do all sorts of things that might make Emily Post—and certainly the other members of your family—smile. Why should you care if your family smiles? If you have to ask that question, then you need to go back and reread this entire volume from cover to cover.

If you do leave your home in order to go to your soul-sucking job, then you know how to be someone others don't hate. You won't be a suck-up. You won't have irritating habits.

If you're out on the road, you won't be a menace.

And if you go anywhere in public, you'll know how to spread the gospel of courtesy. It's not as Earth-shattering as the Gospels according to Matthew, Mark, Luke, and that other one, but it could make this planet a better place to live. And, at the end of the day, isn't that a goal to which all of us should aspire?

Oh, and if you disagree, then go . . . have a super great day anyway.

INDEX